Joseph Conrad's *Under Western Eyes*
Beginnings, Revisions, Final Forms

JOSEPH CONRAD IN 1910.
Drawn by W. H. Caffyn from a photograph by Will Cadby.

Joseph Conrad's
Under Western Eyes:
Beginnings,
Revisions,
Final Forms

Five Essays Edited by
David R. Smith

ARCHON BOOKS ■ Hamden ■ Connecticut

© 1991 David R. Smith. All rights reserved.

First published in 1991 as an Archon Book, an imprint of
The Shoe String Press, Inc., Hamden, Connecticut 06514

The paper used in this publication meets the minimum requirements
of American National Standard for Information Sciences — Perma-
nence of Paper for Printed Library Materials, ANSI Z39.48—1984.
⊗

All illustrations are from Yale University's Beinecke Rare Book and
Manuscript Library and are published with permission.

Library of Congress Cataloging–in–Publication Data

Joseph Conrad's Under Western eyes: beginnings, revisions, final
    forms: five essays /edited by David R. Smith
        p. cm.
        ISBN 0–208–02302–X
        1. Conrad, Joseph, 1857–1924. Under Western eyes. 2.
    Conrad, Joseph, 1857–1924—Criticism, Textual. I. Smith, David
    R., 1923–1990. II. Title: Under Western Eyes.
    PR6005.O4U599 1990   90–35446
    823' .912—dc20   CIP

Contents

Preface

By most estimates *Under Western Eyes* (1911) counts as the last of Conrad's great novels — a cluster that starts with *Lord Jim* (1900) and continues with *Nostromo* (1904) and *The Secret Agent* (1907). Indeed, one could say that it is the novel toward which the others had tended, for it most deeply meditates the peculiarly Conradian conjoining of politics with the problematics of individual identity that had in different ways and with different emphases been the subject of these earlier works — the balance swinging more to the question "How to be?" in the one or toward the matter of politics in the others. But in *Under Western Eyes*, the most autobiographical of these works, Conrad was able to weave these two themes together into a single fabric because there he dealt most directly with his early years when, in fact, politics had profoundly influenced the formation and destiny of his being.

It is this quality that puts *Under Western Eyes* increasingly at the center of Conrad studies, for his Polish and Ukrainian origins and their formative importance have been gradually opened to our Western eyes. It has been a slow and irregular process, given all the political difficulties that have occurred in the wake of World War II; but in post-Stalinist times Western scholars have increasingly had the opportunity to work in Poland and Polish scholars have more recently been able to work in the West — though Zdzisław Najder, a giant among Conradians, was until recently banned from his homeland, being under a death sentence pronounced *in absentia*, a judgment now happily lifted. In any event, as time has passed, Conrad has been regarded less insularly and romantically as a strange phenomenon who had somehow, mysteriously, come to be a master English stylist. He can now be seen more entire, in his various guises and disguises.

By now we know a good deal more about Conrad than we ever did before, at all the stages of his life and career. There has been a quickening outpouring of scholarship over these past three decades: We have witnessed three major biographies, those of Jocelyn Baines (1960), Frederick R. Karl (1979), and Zdzisław Najder (1983), as well as the valuable collections of Polish documents gathered by Najder, *Conrad's Polish Background* (1964) and *Conrad Under Familial Eyes* (1983). And the *Collected Letters*, under the editorship of Frederick Karl and Laurence Davies, are being published, with volume four, which takes us through the writing of *Under Western Eyes*, about to appear. Fortunately, some of the pertinent letters included in that volume have already circulated amongst several of the authors of the present volume, thanks to the generosity of Messrs. Karl and Davies. A concordance of much of Conrad's work, directed by Todd K. Bender, now exists, and there have been, as well, innumerable books and articles about him and his work, many of which have brought valuable insights, new background material, interesting interpretations. Moreover, Conrad's *oeuvre* is in the process of being brought together in its first scholarly edition under the *imprimatur* of the Cambridge University Press.

It was with all this as background that in May 1989 the authors of the five essays in this collection gathered at the California Institute of Technology for a weekend working session on *Under Western Eyes*. The encounter resulted from my having met Keith Carabine in London, where I gave a preliminary version of the work here included. We discovered that we had similar, even overlapping interests, and from the chance of that meeting evolved the idea of a collaboration between the two of us, an idea that further developed into the proposition that brought the five of us together in *une collaboration à cinq*. Each of us was at that moment deeply involved in *Under Western Eyes*. We had, variously, written about the novel, in one case (Eloise Knapp Hay's *The Political Novels of Joseph Conrad*) blazing the trail that led to it, or were in the process of rethinking and writing about it, or in the case of David Leon Higdon and Keith Carabine were engaged in editing it for the Cambridge University Press. All of us were well acquainted with the manuscript "Razumov," some of us with the typescript. But our individual modes of work, our ways of looking at the world, had led us to approach the novel and its antecedents in different, though quite complementary ways. Our methodologies differ as in some cases our conclusions do, yet what most struck me as I thought about bringing us together to produce this group of essays was the ways in which our thinking about *Under Western Eyes* keeps returning to certain issues, which is what gives this collection the coherence of mutual recognitions.

These essays work variously from the manuscript, the typescript, and the finished novel. Keith Carabine uses the textual transformations occurring from manuscript to typescript to discuss some of the major issues we find in the finished novel. I use Conrad's quite personal marginal jottings in the manuscript as indicators of passages deserving special study because they provide keys to understanding Conrad's deep involvement in the novel. David Leon Higdon, using

the typescript as his principal document, attempts to fix
the exact order of the novel's writing and the stages of its
corrections in order to illustrate Conrad's habits of composition and to establish a basis for interpreting the novel.
Eloise Knapp Hay and Roderick Davis both use the printed
text as evidence. Professor Hay considers Conrad's intentions vis à vis the narrator, a point of some interest, and
concludes that from the start the author intended the narrator as a foil, a negative constant against which to compare
the Russians. Roderick Davis' essay focuses on Razumov,
placing him within the philosophical traditions of Russia
and the West and discussing how the novel examines their
contending ideas in light of their adequacy to meet the test
of his bitter experience.

As different as the approaches are, there are interesting comings together, for, whether looking at the physical evidence of the manuscript or reading the bound book,
these readers are struck by similar aspects of the novel, the
gap at its center or its seeming indecisiveness and cross-
purposiveness, though they may wish to explain these matters in different ways — and there are fundamental dis-
agreements. Eloise Knapp Hay and Keith Carabine see Conrad's attitude toward the narrator in quite different lights.
The former takes the author's mounting critique of the cold
and passionless English teacher as a decisive means of allowing Razumov to emerge in a favorable light and by that
means achieving justice for the Russians, which, she feels,
had been Conrad's aim from the start. To the contrary, the
latter attempts to demonstrate *inter alia* that as Conrad's
view of the novel shifted during the course of its composition, the English narrator created difficulties that one can
see Conrad trying to resolve in the corrections and deletions
he makes in the manuscript and typescript, which suggests
a less predetermined view. These differences arise in part,

though only in part, out of methodology, Eloise Knapp Hay starting in this case from the finished product and Keith Carabine working through the process of composition.

That there are differences of opinion is hardly astounding, but these two essays illustrate what I mean by the coherence of mutual recognition because each in its own way finds the novel problematic at the same stress points, as the other essayists included here also do. And that is also hardly astounding, for we have all crossed and crisscrossed the same ground, have ended as explicators of the striking absences and presences in the novel, and despite differences of method, have often turned to much the same evidence. It is this combination of differences and similarities that cause these five pieces to fit so well together.

The five of us had the pleasure of preparing finished drafts of our work and then of coming together to spend a weekend sharing them with one another, their ideal editors, exchanging ideas, agreeing and disagreeing, learning from one another. It was a rare opportunity to have had such a focused and fruitful discussion, rare because it was both serious and joyful. We hope the results will prove as useful to others as they have to those who wrote them.

DRS

David R. Smith died August 31, 1990. I have tried to follow his wishes in attending to the last details of the production of this volume.

G. W. Pigman III

Acknowledgments

Our thanks go to the Beinecke Rare Book and Manuscript Library of Yale University and to the Philadelphia Free Library for permission to cite from, respectively, the manuscript and the typescript of *Under Western Eyes*. We also thank the Joseph Conrad Estate for permission to print material from these two sources as well as to quote from unpublished letters. We print the portrait of Conrad and the photographs of the manuscript with the permission of the Beinecke.

We are grateful to our colleagues George Pigman III, who has generously guided us through the unbending logic of TeX, the formatting software we used to typeset this book, and John Sutherland, for moral support; to David Grether, chairman of the Humanities and Social Sciences Division of the California Institute of Techology, for helping bring the five authors of these essays together.

Contributors

KEITH CARABINE is a Lecturer in English at the University of Kent. He has edited *Nostromo* for Oxford University Press and is coeditor of *Under Western Eyes* for the forthcoming scholarly edition of Conrad's collected works being published by Cambridge University Press. He is also the author of numerous articles on Conrad.

RODERICK DAVIS is Dean of the College of Arts and Sciences of Samford University, Birmingham, Alabama. He is editing *Mirror of the Sea* for the Cambridge University Press edition and has authored a genetic study of *Under Western Eyes* and several articles on Conrad.

ELOISE KNAPP HAY is Professor of English at the University of California, Santa Barbara. She is the author of *The Political Novels of Joseph Conrad* (University of Chicago Press, 1963, 1981) and of *T. S. Eliot's Negative Way* (Harvard University Press, 1982), and numerous articles on Conrad. She is currently completing *Hawthorne and Dickens: A Comparative Study in Cultures.*

DAVID LEON HIGDON, Paul Whitfield Horn Professor at Texas Tech University, is the editor of *Conradiana.* He is the volume editor of *Almayer's Folly* and coeditor of *Under Western Eyes* for the Cambridge edition. He is the author of many articles on Conrad and on nineteenth-century fiction.

At the time of his death DAVID R. SMITH was Professor of Literature at the California Institute of Technology and the executive editor for the Joseph Conrad Society of America and of *Joseph Conrad Today*. He was the author and editor of *Conrad's Manifesto: Preface to a Career* (The Rosenbach Foundation, 1966). He was also the author of articles on Conrad.

Abbreviations

The following frequently cited works will be referred to in the notes and parenthetically in the text using the abbreviations indicated. Where a series of parenthetical citations clearly refer to the same work, only the page number will appear subsequent to the initial notation.

In many cases of dual publication of books in Britain and the United States, the pagination is the same. The Dent Collected edition of Conrad's works (1946–47), for example, has essentially the same pagination as the Dent Uniform Edition of 1923–1924 because it was printed from the same plates, and both editions resemble the Doubleday, Page version of 1923–1924, for the same reason: by providing the plates for those two editions it became the father of one and the grandfather of the other. Many editions and individual volumes were run from those plates, including, surprisingly, the New Directions paperback edition of *Under Western Eyes*, edited by Morton Dauwen Zabel, the first to appear with a scholarly introduction. This is also true of G. Jean Aubry's two volume *Joseph Conrad: Life and Letters*, published in 1927 by Doubleday, Page in New York and Heineman in London. It is equally true of Zdzisław Najder's *Joseph Conrad: A Chronicle*, published by Cambridge University Press and by Rutgers University Press, both in 1983, and of Jocelyn Baines' *Joseph Conrad: A Critical Biography*, by Weidenfeld and Nicolson in London and McGraw-Hill in New York, both in 1960.

APR   Joseph Conrad. *A Personal Record.* Collected
           Edition. London: J. M. Dent and Sons, Ltd.,
           1946. The pagination is the same as for the
           Dent and Doubleday editions of 1923–1924 ex-
           cept that the prefatory material in the earlier
           editions starts at *v* instead of *iii.*

Baines   Jocelyn Baines. *Joseph Conrad: A Critical Bi-
           ography.* London: Widenfeld and Nicolson, New
           York: McGraw-Hill, 1960.

CPB   Zdzisław Najder, ed. *Conrad's Polish Back-
           ground.* Cambridge: Cambridge University
           Press, 1982.

CL   Joseph Conrad. *The Collected Letters.* Ed.
           Frederick R. Karl and Laurence A. Davies.
           Cambridge: Cambridge University Press, Vol. I,
           1983, Vol. II, 1986, Vol. III, 1988.

CUFE   Zdzisław Najder, ed. *Conrad under Familial
           Eyes.* Cambridge: Cambridge University Press,
           1983.

Hay   Eloise Knapp Hay. *The Political Novels of
           Joseph Conrad: A Critical Study.* Chicago: Uni-
           versity of Chicago Press, 1963, 2nd edn., 1981.

Karl   Frederick R. Karl. *Joseph Conrad: The Three
           Lives.* New York: Farrar, Straus and Giroux,
           1979

LBM   *Joseph Conrad: Letters to William Blackwood
           and David S. Meldrum.* Ed. William Blackburn.
           Durham, NC: Duke University Press, 1958.

LG   Joseph Conrad. *Letters from Joseph Conrad:
           1895–1924.* Ed. Edward Garnett. Indianapolis:
           Bobbs-Merrill, 1928.

LL   G. Jean-Aubry. *Joseph Conrad: Life and Let-
           ters.* 2 vols. London: Heinemann, and New York:
           Doubleday, Page, 1927.

Najder   Zdzisław Najder. *Joseph Conrad: A Chronicle.*
            Cambridge: Cambridge University Press; New
            Brunswick, NJ: Rutgers University Press, 1983.
NLL   Joseph Conrad. *Notes on Life and Letters.* Col-
            lected Edition. London: J. M. Dent and Sons,
            Lt., 1946.
UWE   Joseph Conrad. *Under Western Eyes.* Collected
            Edition. London: J. M. Dent and Sons, Ltd.,
            1946. Doubleday, Page, 1924.

Razumov.

I

To begin with I wish to disclaim
the possession of those gifts of imagination and style which would have enabled
my pen to create for the reader the
personality of the man who called
himself, after the Russian custom
Cyril son of Isidor — Kirylo Sidorovitch
— Razumov.

If I have ever had these gifts in
any sort of living form they
have been smo-
thered out of existence a long time
ago under a wilderness of
words. Words as is well known
are

"The Figure Behind the Veil": Conrad and Razumov in *Under Western Eyes*

Keith Carabine

"The subject has long haunted me."

On 6 January 1908, with only the present first chapter of *Under Western Eyes* completed, Conrad outlined the "theme" to Galsworthy: [1]

> He is now writing a story the title of which is "Razumov". Isn't it expressive? I think that I am trying to capture the very soul of things Russian . . . . It is not an easy work but it may be rather good when its done . . . .
>
> Listen to the theme. The Student Razumov (a natural son of Prince K . . . gives up secretly to the police his fellow student, Haldin, who seeks asylum in his rooms after committing a political crime (supposed to be the murder of de Plehve). First movement in St. Petersburg. (Haldin is hanged of course.)
>
> 2nd in Geneve. The student Razumov meeting abroad the mother and sister of Haldin falls in love with that last, marries her and, after a time, confesses to her the part he played in the arrest of her brother.
>
> The psychological developments leading to Razumov's betrayal of Haldin, to his confession of the fact to his wife and to the death of these people (brought about mainly by

1

the resemblance of their child to the late Haldin), form the
real subject of the story.

As far as I'm aware nobody has commented on the
striking disjunction between Conrad's announced intention,
"to capture the very soul of things Russian," which seems,
in this formulation, as he later told Pinker, "so utterly unlike in subject and treatment from anything I have done
before,"[2] and his account of the "real subject of the story"
— betrayal, and the subsequent need either to justify, to
confess or to be understood — which describes "the very
soul" of themes Conradian.

According to the opening pages of the novel, the "very
soul of things Russian" is manifest in three ways: in "the
origin of Mr. Razumov's record" which "is connected with
an *event* . . . the assassination of a prominent statesman";
in the representatively Russian dimensions of Razumov's
story, and in the narrator's commentary upon both the
"record" and the "event" (*UWE*, 7). Thus, the latter we are
assured, is "characteristic of modern Russia in the actual
fact" and "still more characteristic of the moral corruption
of an oppressed society" (*UWE*, 7); and Razumov's "strange
human document" entails, we learn later, "the rendering —
I perceive it now clearly — of the moral conditions ruling
over a large portion of this earth's surface"; "conditions"
characterized, in all manifestations of Russian life, by "cynicism" (*UWE*, 67).[3]

The other, *private* "origin" of Razumov's record Conrad candidly informs us in "A Familiar Preface" — which
was deliberately designed "to explain (in a sense) how I
came to write such a novel"[4] — must be sought in the
life of the novelist "who is the only reality in an invented
world, among imaginary happenings and people. Writing
about them he is only writing about himself" (*APR*, xiii).
Yet, inevitably, Conrad reminds us "the disclosure is not

complete. He remains, to a certain extent, a figure behind a veil: a suspected rather than a seen presence — a movement and a voice behind the draperies of fiction"(*APR*, xiii). In order to glimpse the author's "movement" and to eavesdrop on his "voice" in *Under Western Eyes*, we need, according to Conrad, to trace "the memories" that sustained his "literary life" and to monitor his "discourse with" (in this instance) his Polish "shades"(*APR*, xv). "The real subject" of the novel outlined to Galsworthy — Haldin's disruptive appeal, in the name of the revolution, for Razumov's help, and the latter's betrayal and subsequent confession to the sister — was one that "has long haunted me. Now it must come out."[5] "The inner story"[6] embedded in this "subject" can be located in the problems Conrad encountered as a Pole struggling to establish himself as an English author and can be traced to the charges of "betrayal," "desertion" and "faithlessness" that pursued two of the great decisions of his life, namely to leave Poland, the land his ancestors "had bedewed with their blood" "*Pro patria!*" and to become an *English* novelist(*APR*, 35).[7]

In this essay I attempt to disclose the "figure behind the veil" in all of Razumov's various writings — his "prize essay," his "political confession of faith," his spy report, his final written confession to Natalia, and his personal "record" — and, particularly in the MS of *Under Western Eyes*, all of which are intimately intertwined with Conrad's own life and authorship. I approach the prime document, Razumov's "record," through the MS because it is more patently autobiographical than the novel itself. Moreover, they demonstrate that Conrad's determination to capture "the very soul of things Russian" actually involved, as he slowly realized, an exploration and a reassessment of his troubled, divided feelings with regard to his Polish past and heritage. Razumov's dilemma and his different modes of writing began to refract Conrad's own urgent need to seek "discourse" with, to be understood by and, perhaps, to exorcise, his haunting, inescapable Polish "shades."[8]

Razumov's "prize essay."

Razumov, like his creator, is an "orphan" whose "closest parentage" is defined by his nationality alone, and whose "immense parentage suffered from the throes of internal dissensions . . . he shrank mentally from the fray as a good-natured man may shrink from taking definite sides in a violent family quarrel" (*UWE*, 10–11). Before Haldin's "disruption" he is preoccupied with "examinations" and "the subject of the prize essay. He hankered after the silver medal" offered "by the Ministry of Education" because it provided him a chance to affirm his Russianess and to "claim an administrative appointment of the better sort after he had taken his degree" (*UWE*, 11). Conrad's treatment of Razumov's essay and his anticipated career have received scant critical attention:[9] both can be read, however, as refractions of and commentaries upon, his departure from Poland and upon the difficulties he faced as he struggled to establish himself as an *English* novelist.

Razumov's chosen career represents one of the two alternatives available to Conrad if he had remained in Poland. He could either follow the advice his uncle first offered to him as a mere eleven year old orphan — to acquire "a thorough education" and through "work and determination" master "a profession" such as "an engineer or a technician. . . a doctor or a lawyer" (*CPB*, 35); or as a novitiate of his father's Romantic, Messianic Nationalism, accept Poland as his "faith" and "palm of martyrdom."[10] The former choice, as his uncle continually insisted, would prevent him becoming "a puppet" (of his Nałecz past?) and enable him to become "a useful and worthy person," and a benefit to society (*CPB*, 36): the alternative would either lead to death and martyrdom at the barricades, exile, or, minimally, the ruin of any hopes for a productive career.

In fact the two broad alternatives Conrad rejected when he left Poland in 1874 were followed with fearful symmetry by two other wards of Bobrowski, Conrad's first cousins, Stanisław and Tadeusz Bobrowski, Jr. The latter, Conrad's uncle proudly informed him, passed all his examinations and entered into the service of the Tsarist Government and travelled to Chicago for the great Exhibition of 1894 "in the suite of the heir to the Throne"(*CPB*, 163, 170). Stanisław studied to be a lawyer; and though thought by his guardian "a worthy character," he was also "very presumptious and rather doctrinaire. Possibly . . . in fact ultrademocratic"(*CPB*, 149). In January 1892 Stanisław was arrested and jailed in the Warsaw citadel, "accused of some political or rather social propaganda." According to Bobrowski it was "nothing more than simply a case of unauthorized teaching of artisans — but as there is a tint of nationalism, it becomes complicated"(*CPB*, 162). Not surprisingly Conrad followed the case anxiously; after all Stanisław's awful fate repeated that of Apollo's who was also an ultra-democratic nationalist "imprisoned in the Warsaw Citadel" where "characteristically for our nation," as Conrad told a fellow Pole, "my childhood memories began."[11] The "case," Bobrowski reported, "is devoid of the elementary principles of defense" and "whichever way it goes he is a lost man."[12]

Much ink has been spilt over Conrad's departure from Poland, and his own account of his motives in *A Personal Record*, written some thirty four years after the event, has been severely questioned, by Najder in particular (Naj-

der, 341 ff.). Yet I feel that Conrad, admittedly with the benefit of hindsight (and not least his two cousins' contrasting
fates), crisply formulates in *A Personal Record* what as "an
awakening soul" he may not have understood, while simultaneously he remains true to what he must have glimpsed:
if he had stayed in Poland he could never have worked towards what his father and uncle (in their own eyes at least)
achieved in their different ways — namely "a coherent justifiable personality, both in its origin and in its action," precisely because his debilitating experience with his dying father, together with his uncle's vigorous critique, convinced
him to adapt the words of his father's somber "Christening Song," that *"Poland* — your *Mother"* was most certainly "in her grave."[13] Korzeniowski's *raison d'etre* was,
then, for the son an impossibility. Again the great question
raised by his decision to go to sea — "What reward could
I expect from such a life at the end of my years, either in
ambition, honor or conscience?" *(APR,* 43) — may have the
ring of hindsight: but surely *how to live your life* as a Pole
and as a man, on precisely these terms, dominates both Korzeniowski's and Bobrowski's conflicting credos.[14] (It is also
one of the great themes in Conrad's fiction as the careers
of Kurtz, Jim, Razumov and Heyst testify.) As *A Personal
Record* shows, if he had stayed in Poland there *was* "no
reward . . . either in ambition, honour or conscience" for
the "awakening soul" of the highly strung orphan caught
between the inexorable messianic, Nationalist imperatives
of his father and the prosaic, conciliatory Positivism of his
uncle. Therefore, in ways that he may not have understood
at the time, he chose to be "without people" and "without country" when he took (in a notorious formulation) "a
standing jump out of his racial surroundings and associations" *(APR,* 121).

From this perspective Razumov's pursuit of the silver medal, which is disrupted when "the Revolution sought him out to put to the test his dormant instincts, his half-conscious thoughts . . . by the touch as of some furious and dogmatic religion, with its call to frantic sacrifices" (*UWE*, 294), is a worst case scenario of Conrad's unavoidable fate (one manifested in the trajectories of his father's and Stanisław's tragic careers) if he had stayed in Poland and had tried to pursue a professional career and to adopt his uncle's gradualist politics.[15] In Conrad's self-justifying fantasy version of a fate he avoided, the "sane" orphan Razumov, "living in a period of mental and political unrest," discovers he cannot keep "an instinctive hold on normal, practical, everyday life" (10), because once "the Revolution had sought him out" (194), he fears he will "remain a political suspect all his days . . . . What sort of future could he look forward to?" (71). Razumov's enforced encounters with Haldin and Mikulin oblige him (more directly than his creator), to incarnate and endure "the internal dissensions" of his "immense parentage," which was tainted with "the moral corruption of an oppressed society where the noblest aspirations of humanity, the desire of freedom, *an ardent patriotism* [my emphasis] . . . are prostituted to the lusts of hate and fear, the inseparable companions of an uneasy despotism" (10, 7).

Again from this perspective Razumov's betrayal of Haldin enacts Conrad's guiltiest feelings with regard to the abandonment of the values for which his father, like Haldin, gave his life — "patriotism," belief in God, faith (in Natalia's words) "in the power of the people's will to achieve anything," and self-sacrifice in a vain attempt to escape "the degradation of servitude" and to uproot and sweep out "the absolutist lies" (133).[16]

Razumov's pursuit of the silver medal through the writing of a "prize essay" also intersects with Conrad's own writing career in several interesting ways — all of which are broached in a remarkable passage which Conrad cut from the TS in the spring of 1910. It would have ended Part Third, Chapter 1 where the narrator speculates that "Mr. Razumov looked at" his diary "as a man looks at himself in the mirror, with wonder, perhaps with anguish, with anger or despair . . . formulating to himself reassuring excuses for his appearance marked by the taint of some insidious hereditary disease"(214). (A concise description of Conrad's own latent activity in the novel?) The old teacher reflects on Razumov's writing habits *before* the intrusion of Haldin:

> And there was also in him possibly that habit of depen-
> dence on paper and ink of a man who for years has been
> studying with the fierce perseverance of toil a prisoner
> would display in digging his way out of an obscure dun-
> geon. Mr. Razumov had been trying to escape from the
> obscure state into which he had been born. The pen was
> his principal implement. He had for years, read, thought,
> lived pen in hand fixing his conquered knowledge of facts,
> theories, systems, speculations in the shape of notes. And
> now he was trying perhaps to fix in the familiar way and
> with the idea of serving a practical purpose another kind
> of knowledge — the knowledge of impulses emotions and
> thoughts altogether his own, of complex feelings on a back-
> ground of sombre determination to go on to the bitter end,
> as if life were a book of black science which once opened
> must be read to the last of its futile and accursed pages.[17]

Clearly Conrad had to edit, even if he did not cut, this passage because an older Razumov with a long writing career is hardly consistent with his student youth. These inconsistencies, however, merely serve to highlight the re-markably overdetermined aspects of the sequence: the man looking in this mirror, at this particular moment, as Con-rad must have recognized when he slashed it, is manifestly the unveiled author, whose own writing life was the matrix of his protagonist's.

Even the very imagery rehearses Conrad's descriptions of his own predicament during the composition of "Razumov." Thus in April 1909, only a month before he wrote this sequence, he complained to Stephen Reynolds: "I am pen and ink ridden. It's a nightmare."[18] He was not exaggerating. Since late March 1908 Conrad had found the writing of "Razumov" "horribly difficult": and during the depths of his despair in August 1908 he wailed to Arthur Symonds; "I have been quarrying my English out of a black night, working like a coal-miner in his pit."[19] Also, as with his creation, "the pen was the principal instrument" whereby Conrad would, in Razumov's words, "conquer a name"(*UWE*, 71). "For one has to write in order to live," he wrote 10 March 1896, shortly before he married: "The literary profession is therefore my sole means of support .... I have ventured into this field with . . . the determination to achieve a reputation — . . . I do not doubt my success"(*CL*, I:267).[20] And as his career amply attests, nobody worked with "fiercer determination" than Conrad to leave behind an *oeuvre* that would ensure his "reputation"; and to that end he was fiercely jealous of the need to "protect" his "powers" as he composed "Razumov." "I wrote 'The Black Mate,'" he told Pinker in February 1908, "for no other reason but that I did not want "Razumov" mangled by fools; also to have a free hand with that story. If I can't have a free hand — time — for elaborating my work and freedom from interference I would just have soon stop writing entirely."[21]

In a further intersection, Conrad shares with his protagonist the handicaps he faced as a Pole trying to break out of his "obscure state" in order to conquer a name as an English novelist. Thus to Garnett early in his career (19 June 1896) he lamented: "I have to drag it all out of myself. Other writers have some starting point. Something to catch hold of .... They lean on . . . dialect — or on

tradition — or on history .... while I don't"(*CL*, I:288).
In a similar vein he interrupted the Micawberish flow of
a letter to Pinker, written shortly after he began "Razumov," to lament that unlike his English contemporaries;
"I have no charm, no flow of wit or of facetiousness . . .
I have only a mind a quite different gift from the gift of
the gab. I have no literary tradition even which will help
me to spin phrases" (my emphasis).[22] Within a month of
this letter Razumov, sounding like Conrad, bitterly com-
plains to Haldin that because he was an orphan with no
connections, "I am just a man .... *A man with a mind,*"
who lacks his presumptuous disrupter's relations as "a son,
a brother, a nephew, a cousin" (my emphasis). Hence, he
tells Haldin, whereas "you would think first with or against
your class, your domestic tradition — your fireside prejudices . . . I have no tradition. I have nothing to think
against"(*UWE*, 61). Clearly Razumov's isolated, embattled
state as he struggles to make a "name" intimately connects
at such moments with his creator's despairing sense of the
odds stacked against his isolated intellect and his own career.

Conrad's sympathetic identification with Razumov's
lonely struggles informs the narrator's compassionate assessment of the protagonist's desire to "convert the label
Razumov into an honored name. There was nothing strange
in the student Razumov's wish for distinction. A man's real
life is that accorded to him in the thoughts of other men
by reason of respect or natural love"(*UWE*, 14). Some of
the most moving passages in Conrad's correspondence show
how fully he shared his narrator's sentiments. One example, a letter to his earliest literary mentor, must suffice:
"My dear fellow" he wrote Garnett, "you keep me straight
in my work .... For me you are the reality outside, the expressed thought, the living voice! And without you I would

he told Galsworthy, "trying to catch the spectre, the flying shadow of peace. The great thing is not to break down but there are moments I feel as if my resolution not to break down were weakening."26 These tormented and prophetic words, which repeat the old teacher's formulation concerning mankind's search for "peace," could have been written of and by Razumov, who at this stage in his "impossible existence" has just decided to seek his "formula of peace" by betraying Haldin, only to discover, when he writes his "retrospect," that he is now experiencing "true loneliness .... No human being could bear a steady view of moral solitude without going mad"(39).

The next two passages were elided from the TS in the spring of 1910 and, like the former, concern the generative impulses that persuaded Razumov to keep his "record" and Conrad to write the novel.27 The first follows upon the narrator's reference to the moment when Razumov *began* his "diary proper"— namely "the evening after" he "returned home" from his first interview with Mikulin (UWE, 86):28

All that goes before and forms the basis of my narrative up to this point has been written later on in the fullness of fatal memories as a man sits down to live through again in the bitterness or joy of retrospect some unforgettable period of the past. For this is as Razumov himself remarks somewhere in his diary, the only way of assuring ourselves we have something of our own on this earth. Neither the present nor the future can be said to belong to us with that exclusiveness of possession we have of our past.

The second occurs in the same interview and follows Mikulin's revelation that Haldin, under interrogation did not betray his betrayer, Razumov, and precedes [Razumov's] "feeling of general lassitude" after he learns [from M]ikulin that "Haldin had been hanged at four o'clock [this aft]ernoon"(94) — the inevitable consequences of his
.29

think myself alone in an empty universe"(CL, I:353).23 The author Razumov, of course, in marked contrast to his creator, lacks this solace; and Mikulin, who recruits him to write spy reports, *ensures* his protege's appalling isolation.

The most intimate correlation between Razumov's writing career and Conrad's can be seen in the changes wrought upon the protagonist by Haldin's intrusion. After Haldin leaves his room to go to certain arrest and death, Razumov "muttered sourly — It's done .... and now to work"(64). But he is now so obsessed by Haldin that "his mind hovered on the borders of delirium. He heard himself saying 'I confess,' as a person might do on the rack"(65). Thoughts of confession and of "betrayal!" ensure "there could be no question of doing useful work"(71). Now "the scattered pages of his notes and small piles of books" appear to him "a mere litter of blackened paper — dead matter — without significance or interest"(68). Henceforth he will be unable to use the pen academically "to conquer facts, theories, systems."

Razumov's inability to do "useful work" leading to a successful career in the Tsarist bureaucracy may be construed as Conrad's belated reply to his guardian's melioristic plans both for his own and Poland's future. More importantly, however, Haldin's disruption means that a "public" life is no longer possible and Razumov, therefore, for the first time in his life, is driven into himself by his secret thoughts of betrayal and confession, which trigger two new forms of self expression, the five aphoristic lines of what Mikulin calls "a sort of political confession of faith," and, afterwards, his personal "record." (I will return to the "political confession" towards the end of my essay.)

This new shift in Razumov's life and his resort to autobiography, which subserves and shapes "another kind of knowledge," and in turn forms the basis of Conrad's novel, parallels his own shift from a mariner who recorded "entries in my log book," and who was fascinated by "the force, precision and imagery of technical language" true to the "real aspect of the things" sailors "see in their trade," to a novelist who "descends within himself" and who strives "by the power of the written word to make you hear, to make you feel . . . to make you *see!*"[24] And, more particularly, Razumov's shift matches Conrad's abandonment of *Chance* in order to begin "such a novel as *Under Western Eyes*," whose "subject" "must come out." "Living with memories," he told Cunninghame Graham on 7 October 1907, less than two months before he began "Razumov," "is a cruel business. I who have a double life peopled only by shadows growing more precious as the years pass — know what that is" (*CL*, III:491). Conrad dramatizes the "cruel business" of trying to live "a double life peopled by shadows" through the wretched case of Razumov who permits him to "discourse" and grapple with new "impulses . . . and complex feelings" that *Chance* could not accommodate. Indeed from this point of view *Under Western Eyes*, the first fiction set in the land of his birth, can be said to return to and to investigate the ur-story behind all his tales of betrayal, mixed loyalties and confession.

"The very secret . . . of that record's existence."

When Conrad returned to the TS in the spring of 1910 he carefully erased the autobiographical traces; hence the "figure behind the veil" is more discernible there than in the novel. Out of an abundance of riches I want to concentrate on three sequences that enable us to glimpse that apparition, all of which refer to the period *before* Razumov began his "record." They all disclose "how" and why

---

Razumov came to tackle his new "subject," and they all suggest how his "new kind of knowledge," sponsored by Haldin's "disruption," is inextricably intertwined with his author's "complex feelings" about, and "discourse with" his Polish past. My first quotation runs together material from the novel with material found only in the holograph a follows immediately upon the narrator's initial attemp fathom why Razumov should have kept his record in first place:[25]

It is inconceivable that he should have wished an man eye to see it. A mysterious impulse of human comes into play here . . . . There must be a wonderful ing power in mere words since so many men have us for self-communion. Being myself a quiet individu it that what all men are really after is some for haps only some formula of peace. Certainly they out for it at the present day. What sort of p Sidorovitch Razumov expected to find in the record it passeth my understanding to guess.

The fact remains he has written it . . . tuations of his feelings all the perplexities short all the profound trouble of his exist with a terrible minuteness of self examin with long speculative passages in a decl

No wonder the first paragraph sur Conrad later acknowledged in his "A the narrator serviced his own "effo passions, prejudices and even from Most crucially the old English tea psychological necessity, a means himself from the "profound trou sponsored by his passionate er ries of his unavoidable Polish the retained passage shows, men") and bleaches both Ra rad's own "impossible exist

upon
tion,
the la
from M
this aft
betraya

This momentary relaxation of fibre is noted with that haunting fidelity of remembered sensation which is such a remarkable characteristic of Mr. Razumov's record.

This is the best place to say (now the time of my personal contact with Mr. Razumov is drawing near) that I am inclined to think that we have in this characteristic the true explanation — the very secret so to speak — of that record's existence. The haunting fidelity . . . . Few of us are consciously aware of the great part the capacity to forget plays in the successful conduct of our lives. Where that is wanting the very sanity of our existence stands endangered. I am not alluding here to the forgetfulness of facts. On the contrary, the memory of these is very useful; they make indeed the sum of our wisdom. I am thinking here of another order of memories. Haunting fidelity . . . . It may be that when Mr. Razumov seized the pen it was with the intention of building up in written words a resting place for his remembered sensations to the end that they should cease haunting him in all their force. It does not require the animosity of an old man and weary teacher of languages to discover that words are but the grave of all that makes a thought wonderful and an emotion poignant. Involved in the commonplace associations of speech, thought becomes acceptable to the commonplace world and emotion bearable to the relieved soul.

When Conrad read over these passages after "the horrible nightmare of my long illness," during which "the very sanity of" *his* "existence" had stood endangered, they must have proved unbearable to contemplate.[30] After all, the characters of the novel had invaded his psychotic life: "the MS," Jessie records, "complete but uncorrected. . . lays [sic] on a table at the foot of the bed and he lives mixed up in the scenes and holds converse with the characters" (*LBM*, 192).[31] And after all, as his very breakdown and the existence of the MS proved, he had always been "one of the few," like Razumov, who was not only unable "to forget," but one who was "haunted " by "fatal memories" of the

"unforgettable period of his past." The conclusion is irresistible that Conrad, like his creation, "seized the pen . . .
with the intention of building up . . . a resting place for
his remembered sensations to the end they should cease
from haunting him in all their force." "Seized the pen"
even though he knew that "the stirring up these dead"
whether in "Razumov" or in the early "Polish" "Reminiscences" was "a silly enterprise . . . being a somewhat
ghoulish one."[32] Seized the pen, perhaps, with the courage
born of desperation, yet also acting upon his deepest creative belief that "the artist descends within himself, and
in that lonely region of stress and strife finds the terms of
his appeal."[33] Both Conrad's descent into his "own private
little hell" and the potential damage to his psychic life of
this "ghoulish" self-fathoming are, perhaps, imaged when
Razumov retrieves "the book of his compromising record"
to deliver it to Natalia. It "was kept in a locked drawer,
which he pulled out violently, and did not even trouble to
push back afterwards" (*UWE*, 357). Razumov no longer feels
the need at this point to push back the drawer because he
has confessed to Natalia, his "record" attempts to justify
his behavior, and he is about to confess to the revolutionaries. There are to be no more secrets; he wants his life,
as it was before Haldin's disruption, to become "a public
thing."

Razumov's possession of his past is "exclusive" in two
senses: his betrayal of Haldin is known only to himself and
to a few Tsarist officials, and, more importantly, only he
knows what it is "to live with Haldin," who becomes a dark
double and takes possession of his inner life — especially
after he has agreed to be recruited as a Tsarist double agent
by the slyly solicitous Mikulin. This decision serves to render his existence completely false and ensures he becomes
increasingly bitter and more isolated the longer he lives in

his "prison of lies"(*UWE*, 363). Conrad's possession of his
past was also "exclusive": he knew, as his protagonist was
about to discover, that "Living with memories is a cruel
business. I who have *a double life* one of them peopled by
shadows . . . know what that is" (my emphasis). Unfortunately the "memories" that *possessed* him were "of another
order," of a time and place as removed from his English
family and reading public, as the (allegedly) Russian events
were from his English narrator, who bewails "that my very
real sympathy had no standpoint . . . . It was, if I may say
so, the want of experience"(*UWE*, 112). Conrad could not,
therefore, readily share his "double life" with his family and
friends. "I can't think of Poland," he told a fellow Pole, "It
feels too bad, bitter, painful. It would make life unbearable"(*CUFE*, 201). As Conrad told Garnett, though he has
"always wanted to write something" about his memories
of Polish life for his son Borys so as "to save all this from
the abyss a few years longer. . . probably he wouldn't care.
What's Hecuba to him or he to Hecuba." Conrad did not
complete Hamlet's meditation upon the Player King's im-
passioned rendering of Priam's lament for his dead queen
— "that he should weep for her" — because he felt, as the
last of the Korzeniowskis, that he wept alone. So in January 1900 he proposed — because "Tempi passati!" — to
"Let them go"(*CL*, II:247).

But, of course, Conrad could not let them go because,
to adapt Natalia's poignant remark to Razumov, he understood that "it was only in himself that he could find
all that was left of his parents' generous souls"(*UWE*, 346)
and they would not cease haunting him. Conrad's attempt
"to save all this from the abyss" and his related decision
to explore the psychological, familial and historical origins
of his "double life" constitute "the true explanation — the
very secret" of the "existence" of *Under Western Eyes and*

of its unusual "treatment." Both Razumov's "record" and
Under Western Eyes can be traced to Conrad's own "fatal memories" of his "unforgettable" Polish past, and to
his deeply ambivalent attitude to and reassessment of his
"race and family." More particularly, as the *context* of the
second quotation indicates, "the very secret" of Razumov's
diary relates to his attempt to come to terms with his "betrayal" of Haldin, who magnanimously refused to implicate
him in the assassination of "De P—" and thereby compromise and, perhaps, destroy him in turn. In an exact
parallel, Conrad's acknowledgement in "A Familiar Preface" that "One's literary life must turn frequently for sus-
tenance to memories and seek discourse with the shades"
(*APR*, xv), follows hard upon his recollection that he broke
"away from my origins under a storm of blame from every
quarter which had the merest right to an opinion" about
"my allegiance" (xiv). Conrad's formulation here, as so often in *A Personal Record*, is urbanely sly ("merest right")
about his accusers; in keeping, I might add, with his pose,
maintained, as in this instance, against the grain of the very
evidence he himself provides, that he was "by no means
anxious" when he became a novelist "to justify my existence" (94). All the evidence we can canvass — the MS, his
own statements about the relationships between the art
and the life, the psychological imperatives that drove him
to plumb "fatal memories," his close identification during
the long composition of the novel with Razumov's predicament and with his writings — all combine to confirm that
"the very secret," the informing secret of "such a novel as
Under Western Eyes," was indeed his need to "discourse"
with his Polish "shades," and to build up "a resting place
for his remembered sensations to the end they should cease
haunting him in all their force." [34]

Razumov's Spy Report: An "Extraordinary Occupation."

Razumov is not a good spy. Indeed because his inner life is so crowded ("Every word uttered by Haldin lived in Razumov's memory. They were like haunting shapes; they could not be exorcised" [167]), and because his encounters with the revolutionaries lubricate his scorn and, thereby, threaten his own exposure, he even forgets "why I am here"(289). In an elegant irony, his decision to begin his first and last spy report, is prompted by his rankling thoughts about that "violent pamphleteer clamouring for revolutionary justice," Julius Laspara, who requests him to "write something for us"(285, 287). Frenziedly, Razumov remembers, "Write! Must write! . . . That's why I'm here"(288–89). Once he begins to compose, however, he reflects, "Extraordinary occupation I am giving myself up to" (291). This "extraordinary occupation," once again, intercepts and refracts Conrad's own predicament, preoccupations and purposes as he gave himself up to his novel.

As he sits beneath "the exiled effigy of the author of the *Social Contract*," he thinks of his report as "writing which has to be done"(291–92). Razumov's "own social contract" as Aaron Fogel has observed, "is his forced writing," an image of Conrad's sense that writing is "an oblique form of slavery."[35] This identification can hardly be doubted because, tragically, the writing of "Razumov" bound Conrad to a wheel of fire: the compulsion to engage and reshape his "fatal memories" threatened his very sanity and also became, during the twenty-five months he spent on the novel and his autobiography, his only *capital* as he strove to keep his family and endured the awful strain of having to produce regular "batches" of holograph against deadlines and debts looming ever larger. Thus Conrad lamented, the "pressure grew from day to day instead of getting less"

— hastening his estrangement from Pinker and his own breakdown.[36]

Curiously, given that Razumov is poised, within hours, to confess, his spy report does not have to be written. His decision, rather, reflects his stubborn determination to act out his assigned role of spy reporter to prove that he does not have (and could not have) "A conventional conscience" (288). He tries to consider the spy report "the first-fruit of my mission" (316), during which "he had argued himself into new beliefs" (246); beliefs designed to convince himself that both his betrayal and his "mission" were justified by "the visionary and criminal babble of revolutionaries" (248), who therefore positively invited his systematic unmasking. From this angle Razumov's spy report can be construed as an extreme manifestation of Conrad's own need to "justify his existence" as he defiantly — and perhaps, like his protagonist in "a mental atmosphere of gloomy and sardonic reverie" (246) — defends his rejection of his parents' sacrifice by exposing their naïveté and folly. Like the Russian revolutionaries in the novel, his parents were "inspired" and his father, like Haldin, dreamt "of being the chosen Apostle of the people"; but they also failed to recognize that their heroic patriotic activity may have been sponsored by a despairing inability to work within the conditions imposed by "the irremediable life of the earth as it is."[37]

The spy report, therefore, represents the opposite pole to the various modes of confession in the novel which are designed to reconcile Razumov to his existence. Appropriately, therefore, "the flimsy batch" of the report (in contrast to the batches Conrad forwarded to Pinker that constitute the novel itself) is described as "scribbling" (291). This kind of writing is purely negative, and self-destructive, attempting, in Razumov's words "to confirm myself in my contempt and hate for what I betrayed" (369). The problem for both

Conrad and Razumov was how to shed the crippling aspects of this defiant identity — falsehood, scorn, self-loathing, and isolation — and how to build "a resting place," while retaining, in the words of "A Familiar Preface," "a coherent and justifiable personality both in its origin and its action"(*APR*, xxi). The two remaining kinds of writing in the novel that I have not discussed, namely Razumov's "political confession of faith" and his written confession to Natalia attempt to achieve such an identity.

Razumov's "political confession" and his written confession to Natalia.

> History not Theory.
> Patriotism not Internationalism.
> Evolution not Revolution.
> Direction not Destruction.
> Unity not Disruption.(66)

Razumov's political credo, "crystallized by the shock of his contact with Haldin"(67), can be read as Conrad's precarious attempt to balance the competing ideological traditions of his Polish heritage in relation to the painful accusations of betrayal he endured. "Evolution," "Direction" and "Unity" are the values of Bobrowski, "History" and "Patriotism" of Korzeniowski.

Publicly, Conrad always maintained, in the teeth of the historical evidence, but in keeping with the extremely idealistic tenets of his father's Polish romantic Nationalism, that the beliefs of the Old Polish Commonwealth were "sanctioned by popular tradition, by ideas of intelligent loyalty, of devotion, of political necessity."[38] These beliefs were therefore, like England's, directed, unified and historical. Privately, however, Conrad acknowledged that "with us religion and patriotism go hand in hand"(*CL*, I:174), and admitted that "I always, from the age of fourteen, disliked the Christian religion, its doctrines, ceremonies and festivals. Presentiment that some day it will work my undoing, I suppose"(*CL*, II:468). Razumov's credo, from this angle, masks Conrad's engagement with and rejection of the mystic messianic elements in his father's "Patriotism." Moreover his version of the fate that the sins of the father would have visited upon the son, if like Razumov he had remained a citizen of the Russian Empire, contradicts his public stance. "Disruption" and "Disunity," rather, followed in his father's wake as they did in Haldin's and sponsored "moments of revolt which stripped off me," like Razumov, his fictional surrogate, "some of my simple trust in the government of the universe."[39]

Again, briefly, the same ambivalence permeates the old Englishman's onslaught on "the Russian character. The illogicality of their attitude, the arbitrariness of their conclusions, the frequency of the exceptional"(4). This insistence (particularly marked in Part First of the novel) that the characters in the novel are a race apart, tallies with Conrad's own polemic against Russia in "Autocracy and War"; and both, moreover, lean heavily upon his father's deeply prejudiced, anguished depiction of Muscovite "corruption" in his diatribe, "Poland and Muscovy." According to Korzeniowski, "the aim of Muscovy's development is to bring to a standstill all progress of humankind," and "to smear her own deceit over the rest of humanity"(*CUFE*, 77, 79). In keeping with Conrad's espousal of his father's attack on the negations inherent in Muscovy, Razumov's tragedy is truly Russian: because a blind, mystic "autocracy and nothing else . . . has moulded her institutions" she has no "history" and is therefore incapable of "Evolution . . . Direction . . . Unity."[40] Thus he desperately claims a "history" and a set of (western) values, which an autocracy inherently denies and systematically opposes.

Clearly, both Razumov's credo and Conrad's sly use of his English narrator to voice Korzeniowski's heated objections, permeate the subject and the unusual "treatment" of *Under Western Eyes*. Crucially they also allow Conrad privately to justify himself to his Polish "shades" because, at such moments in the novel, he strives to be true to what he calls in *A Personal Record* "the inner voice" of his Polish "conscience"; "fidelity to a special tradition may last through the events of an unrelated existence" — even that of an English novelist(35-36).

Yet of course, as Razumov's "record" amply attests, Haldin's (and Korzeniowski's) self-sacrificial "Patriotism" leads to a "shambles," destroys Razumov's chosen career as an essayist and Tsarist bureaucrat, and earns both the protagonist's and the old teacher's (and Bobrowski's) scorn. Even so, and this is typical of Conrad's ambivalence, he does not finally refute, as Razumov's written confession to Natalia shows, either his father's heroic martyrdom or his ideals. Thus Razumov admits in the last words "I shall ever write," "In giving Viktor Haldin up, it was myself, after all, whom I betrayed most basely." And "after all," he continues (in a passage, incidentally, Conrad added *after* his breakdown) "it is they [the revolutionists] and not I who have the right on their side! — theirs is the strength of invisible powers"(361).[41] Conrad had already encountered and registered this "right" at the end of the first "Reminiscence" (written in September 1908) when after recounting the exile of his parents, he acknowledges that "I did not understand the tragic significance of it at the time"(*APR*, 24). When he began to give his full attention to the novel in the early months of 1909, after an extended *impasse,* "the tragic character" floods "the whole story . . . and . . . the march of its events"(*APR*, vii) culminating in both their confessions and their last desperate tributes to the higher justice of their respective haunting "shades."[42]

Even so the confessions of author and protagonist fall short of a full endorsement of either the activities or beliefs of their joint "Shades." "So be it," the revised sequence continues, "Only don't be deceived, Natalia Victorovna, I am not converted. Have I then the soul of a slave? No! I am independent — and therefore perdition is my lot"(361–62).

"Invisible powers" may have "the right on their side," but "the right" is terribly difficult to fulfill as both the whole story and the history of Poland's just struggle for national independence sadly demonstrate. Moreover "the right," incarnated in Haldin, "a political saint"(61), whose "life," like Korzeniowski's, "had been sincere and perhaps . . . its moral sufferings profound, its last act a true sacrifice"(164) can also be in thrall to "folly . . . and illusion"(376) and can degenerate, as Haldin's tormented words to Razumov prove, into mysticism and arbitrariness: "The Russian soul that lives in all of us . . . has a mission . . . or else why should I have been moved to do this — reckless — like a butcher — in the middle of all these innocent people — scattering death — I! . . . I wouldn't hurt a fly!"(22). And even when the "right" is incarnated in souls as pure and redemptive as Natalia and Conrad's mother, who "represent nobly the ideal of" Russian and of "Polish womanhood"(*APR*, 29),[43] nonetheless they risk surrendering their lives to "folly . . . and illusion," thereby rendering themselves "defenseless"(*UWE*, 360, 376).

These late corrections surely disclose the "figure behind the veil." "Invisible powers," as Conrad's own breakdown revealed, cannot be appeased precisely because they *are* "invisible," so their response, like that of the gods to mankind's hapless prayers, cannot finally be known; the struggle for independence, therefore, invites "undoing" and "perdition." (From this perspective the writing of both *Under Western Eyes* and *A Personal Record* is symptomatic of the "survivor guilt" that Freud diagnosed in himself after the death of his own father.)[44] Again, because "words are the great foes of reality" (*UWE*, 3) and "the grave of all that makes a thought wonderful and an emotion poignant," even the sincerest expressions of love and of filial devotion, like the last words Razumov "shall ever write" (364), may prove "incoherent" (357); and, therefore, may sabotage any search for "some form or formula of peace." Hence we should not be surprised by the "complex feelings" of defensiveness, self-pity, piety, despair and defiance, manifest in Razumov's and Conrad's "personal records."

Razumov's and his creator's confessions, therefore, though they crave forgiveness, do not promise conversion (as most confessions do). Rather they are attempts to build up "in written words a resting place for . . . remembered sensations to the end that they should cease haunting . . . in all their force"; attempts that confess from the outset their own inadequacy. Yet, in one final twist, the "book . . . . sent to me [Natalia] wrapped up in my veil," is a perfect image of that uneasy balancing, in both their "records," of their conflicting needs to justify their actions and to come to terms with "the new kind of knowledge" of "emotions and . . . complex feelings" their actions sponsored. In this respect Natalia's response, as the first reader, strives to justify the "book's" bitter wisdom: "And while you read it," she tells the narrator and, thereby, the readers, "please remember that I *was* defenseless" (376). Natalia's testimony to the power of both Razumov's "book" and the novel Conrad sends via his English narrator to both his invisible Polish shades and to his living Edwardian and Polish publics, acknowledges that both records create "something living still," "something authentic" (375, 191). In marked contrast to the levity of Laspara's revolutionary journal, the *Living Word*, in which "Any subject could be treated in the right spirit and for the ends of social revolution" [287], the "personal records" of Conrad and Razumov are "living" forms(3). "Living" because they share similar origins — "the dormant seeds of her brother's words" (358) in Razumov's case and the "discourse with" his Polish "shades" in Conrad's; "living" because both try to negotiate, mould and "explain," in the anguished words of *A Personal Record*, "the intimate alliance of contradictions in human nature which makes love itself wear at times the desperate shape of betrayal" (36); "living" because they strive for "haunting fidelity" to the "internal dissensions" within both their race and families and within themselves. They are both, finally, faithful, even at the risk of "perdition," to their precariously held identities as *homo* and *scriptor duplex*; faithful to the tensions and divisions their very names embody — Józef Teodor Konrad Korzeniowski (coat of arms Nałecz and pen name Joseph Conrad) and Cyril son of Isidor — Kirylo Sidorovich Razumov.[45]

NOTES

[1] *LL*, II:64–65.

[2] A.L.S. 13 Sept. 1911. Several of the letters in this essay to Pinker and others, from 1908 on, are unpublished and are quoted with the permission of the Henry W. and Albert A. Berg Collection, The New York Public Library. The author would like to thank Dr. Lola Szladits and her staff for their unfailing courtesy and co-operation.

[3] The narrator disclaims any "comprehension of the Russian character" (p. 4) and claims to be bemused by Razumov's "record." This use of a persona alerts the reader to the author ("the figure behind" the mask) who clearly knows far more about "things Russian" and is more deeply involved in the "real subject," than his cannily chosen teller.

[4] 13 Sept. 1911, Berg. This important and neglected letter confirms that "A Familiar Preface" — the finest meditation on the relationship between his life and his art Conrad ever wrote — is of special relevance to *Under Western Eyes*, the most autobiographical of his fictions. Conrad wrote the "Preface" in the summer of 1911, the novel was published on 5 Oct. 1911.

[5] 7 Jan. 1908, A.L.S. Berg. In the letter of the previous day to Galsworthy, quoted at the beginning of this paper, the same compulsive note is struck: "I had to write it" (*LL*, II:65).

[6] 7 Oct. 1908, A.L.S. Berg. In this letter to Pinker Conrad promises that his proposed "Reminiscences" (which became *A Personal Record*) will ensure "the inner story of most of my books will come out . . . a sort of literary confession as to the sources as well as to the aims. I have been thinking of a title something like 'The Art and the Life.'" His formulations anticipate "A Familiar Preface."

[7] Conrad's Polishness ensured these haunting charges would inevitably attend his decision to become an English novelist because his father, as even Bobrowski reminded his nephew, "did serve his country with his pen"; and Poles of all persuasions were bound to query why he wrote about Dutch dreamers living in Eastern seas, such as Almayer, when he could "use his talent

to glorify Poland's name . . . and depict in his novels the unhap-
piness of his native land" ("Joseph Conrad in Cardiff" by Witold
Chwalewik in *CUFE*, p. 175). As we know the inevitable occurred when he was accused, in 1899, by Eliza Orzeszkowa of betrayal, of draining away "the life blood of the nation" by writing
"popular and lucrative novels in English" (*ibid.*, p. 187). Even
Conrad's father, who excoriated the back-sliding bourgeoisie for
their selfish neglect of the "holy" cause of Poland's freedom,
could not have advanced the case for the prosecution more bitterly; and to his son's sense of the matter, as *A Personal Record*
makes abundantly clear, more unjustly. Polish commentators,
especially, trace Conrad's obsessive interest in betrayal, guilt,
and loyalty to their prominence in Polish Romantic literature
and to his own guilt over his departure and his career as an English novelist. Readers interested in this huge and controversial
subject should begin with the documents gathered by Z. Najder in *CPB*, and in *CUFE*. Gustav Morf's *The Polish Heritage
of Joseph Conrad* (Haskell House, New York, 1965) (first published, 1930) is a pioneering, overstated work in which "doubles"
of Conrad and reworkings of his father abound. More balanced
is Andrej Busza's "Conrad's Polish Literary Background and
Some Illustrations of the Influence of Polish Literature on his
Work," *Antemurale*, 10 (1966), 109-247. For Conrad's father see
C. Milosz, "Apollo N. Korzeniowski," *Mosaic*, 6:4 (1973), 121–
140, (originally published in *Kultura*, Paris, Feb. 1956, pp. 60–
80). For "Western" accounts of Conrad's Polish background see
Hay and also Robert F. Hodges, *The Dual Heritage of Joseph
Conrad* (The Hague: Mouton, 1967).

[8] Inevitably, my approach sidelines the ostensible subject of
the novel. For a fine account of how "In Razumov's own nature,
Conrad figures the central dilemma and tragedy of Russian life,"
see Hay, p. 290.

[9] The exceptions are Avrom Fleishman, "Speech and Writing in Under Western Eyes," *Joseph Conrad: A Commemoration*, ed. N. Sherry (London: Macmillan, 1976), pp. 119–128, and
Penn R. Szittya, "Metafiction: The Double Narration in *Under
Western Eyes*," *English Literary History*, 48 (1981), 817–840. I

came across Szittya's fine argument after I had finished my essay: "The diary is a symbolic counterpoint to the essay; one is public, the other private; Haldin destroys the writing of the one, but generates the writing of the other" (p. 821).

The TS alone provides the title of the essay, "The Civil Reform of Peter the Great" (see Higdon's essay in this volume for details, p. 72). Razumov's attitude to the first Tsar to look to the West for inspiration is not described. Razumov's chosen subject suggests that his aims and political beliefs are more confused than he realizes. Thus, on the one hand he believes, like Peter, in "Civil Reform," yet (also like Peter) he thinks "absolute power should be preserved" (p. 35). This contradiction riddled Tsarist politics from Peter's reign until the last of the Tsars, Nicholas II (1894–1917).

[10] Poem by Apollo Korzeniowski, "To my son in the 85th year of Muscovite oppression, a song for the day of his christening," *CUFE*, p. 32. His son's christening, for Apollo, was clearly the beginning of a strenuous novitiation into an underground fellowship of Poles: "Baby son, tell yourself / You are without land, without love, / without country, without people, / while *Poland — your Mother* is in her grave" (p. 33).

[11] "You wish and expect," Bobrowski writes, "to have some definite news of Stanisław," (5/17 Oct. 1892, p. 168); 9 June 1897, in *CL*, I:358. Korzeniowski was imprisoned in the Warsaw Citadel (the symbol of Russian oppression for Poles) in 1862. Among the momentous charges brought against him was that "he had organized in Zytomierz communal prayers for the people who had been killed in Warsaw by the Russians during the political demonstrations" (*CUFE*, p. 63).

[12] *CPB*, 5/17 Oct. 1892, p. 168. Stanisław was eventually "taken to St. Petersburg to serve . . . a year and half in prison" (p. 172). The relatively mild sentence (by Tsarist standards) was no consolation to Bobrowski because his nephew "could never become either a government official, a solicitor, or a notary — not even in Kamchatka!! His whole life has gone off the rails" (p. 168). The parallels between Stanisław's fate and ruined future and Razumov's and between the political condi-

tions that skewered their careers hardly need stressing. Compare for example Razumov's reflections on his future (on a more serious charge than Stanisław's teaching of artisans) to Bobrowski's above: "Razumov saw himself shut up in a fortress, worried, badgered, perhaps ill-used. He saw himself deported by an administrative order, his life broken, and robbed of all hope" (p. 21).

[13] "A Familiar Preface," *APR*, p. xxi; *CUFE*, p. 33; Keith Carabine, review of Najder, ed. *Conrad under Familial Eyes*, in *Conradiana*, 18 (1986), 48-59.

[14] For Korzeniowski, see his "Christening Poem" and the letters gathered by Najder in *CUFE*; for Bobrowski's melioristic political hopes, *ibid.*, pp. 35-36). Both the latter's Positivist views on man's duties to his society and his critique of Korzeniowski's messianic Nationalism are firmly outlined in his fine letter to Conrad, 28 Oct./9 Nov. 1891, *CPB*, pp. 152–56.

[15] Cf. Joseph Dobrinsky, *The Artist in Conrad's Fiction: A Psychocritical Study* (U.M.I. Research Press, Ann Arbor, 1989): "It is as if Conrad were saying . . . 'This is the worst possible representation of the case, and yet . . . .' " (p. 95).

[16] The correspondences between Korzeniowski's "Red" essentially "Populist nationalism" and Haldin's "Populist" beliefs are historically grounded. See Peter Brock, "Polish Nationalism" in Peter F. Sugar and Ivo J. Lederer, eds, *Nationalism in Europe* (Seattle and London: University of Washington, 1969), pp. 310-372. Such correspondences greatly complicate both the identification of the sources of *Under Western Eyes* and our application of them. Thus Conrad's sardonic depiction of the drunken peasant, Ziemianitch, hailed by Haldin as a "bright spirit" (p. 18) "with an "extraordinary . . . sense of the necessity of freedom" (p. 56), can be read both as a satire of such enthusiastic depictions of the revolutionary terrorist as, Stepniak's *Career of a Nihilist* (London: Scott, 1889), and of the Garnetts-inspired, liberal Edwardian admiration for the Russian revolutionary "soul," and as one manifestation of Conrad's (and Bobrowski's) critique of Korzeniowski's romantic heralding of the people's virtues.

[17] TS, "G" batch, p. 15; "Razumov," pp. 859–60. The TS

is in the Philadelphia Free Library and the holograph is in The Beinecke Manuscript and Rare Book Collection at Yale. The TS is composed of the "clean copy of Razumov," typed in the fall of 1908 (comprising pp. 3–160 of *UWE*) and thereafter of unpaginated batches of TS, lettered 'A' through 'T', plus, in holograph, a rewrite of the end. I thank both libraries and the Joseph Conrad estate for permission to quote from the MS. For further details, at every stage of my summary remarks on the composition of *Under Western Eyes*, check David Leon Higdon's full description of the provenance and composition of the TS in this volume. Our essays should be read as complementary exercises. "To go on to the bitter end," in keeping with Conrad's latent self-justification, is a bitter version of Bobrowski's "motto": "I have gone through a lot, I have suffered over my fate and the fate of my family and my Nation, and perhaps just because of these sufferings and disappointments I have developed in myself this calm outlook on the problem of life, whose motto, I venture to say, was, is and will be 'usque ad finem'" ["until the end"] (*CPB*, p. 155). Stein develops a more hopeful variant: "That was the way. To follow the dream, and again to follow the dream — and so — ewig — usque ad finem . . . " (*Lord Jim*, Chapter 20). Patusan is a land fit for Romance: dreams are incapable of fulfillment in both the Poland of *A Personal Record* and the Russia of *Under Western Eyes*.

[18] 14 April 1909, A.L.S. Berg.

[19] 2 April 1908, to Pinker, Berg; 29 August, 1908, *LL*, II:84. Conrad wrote the present Part First of *Under Western Eyes* in a little over three months (early December, 1907 to mid-March, 1908). Until the spring of 1909, however, as his unpublished letters and the MS indicate, his progress was slow and patchy. The main hiatus occurred between September 1908 and mid-January 1909. "The clean copy" (30 Sept. 1908, A.L.S. Berg) Conrad had typed in late September and October 1908 ends just as Razumov is poised to reenter the Geneva narrative (Part Second, Chapter IV, p. 160). Galsworthy read this "clean copy" and was told by Conrad, "What you see is the residue of very many pages now destroyed" (30 Nov. 1908, *LL*, II:90). Conrad's

biographers have wrongly assumed that this letter indicates that he had finished Part Second of the novel; in fact, he did not finish this part until late March 1909! For details check Higdon.

[20] Jean Aubry's translation of this Polish letter reads "with the firm resolution to make a name" (*LL*, I:185).

[21] 7 Jan. 1908, and 13? Feb., to Pinker, A.L.S. Berg.

[22] 14 Jan. 1908, A.L.S. Berg. The root of Razumov, *razum* in Russian, means "mind," "intellect," "reason."

[23] 20 April, 1897. This is perhaps the main "temperamental" reason behind Conrad's elaborate fictional strategies, which are "aimed essentially at the intimacy of a personal communication" (14 July 1923, *LL*, II:317).

[24] *The Mirror of The Sea* (1906), Dent Collected Edition (1946), pp. 88, 21; "Preface" to *The Nigger of the "Narcissus."*

[25] *UWE*, p. 5, "Razumov," p. 9. The material in brackets is from the latter. It could have been cut either in December 1907, when Conrad habitually revised the batches of TS Pinker returned (called "the intermediate TS") or, more likely, when he prepared the latter for "the clean copy" typed in September/October, 1908. The sequence, perhaps, echoes a striking passage from Bobrowski's Memoirs: "And finally myself, a convinced doctrinaire, deeply confident of the inflexible and unchanging rights and duties of the mind, of critical judgement and free will which make a man master of his own fate and history; I reject all side influences issuing from emotions and passions and from other people; through clear thinking I have arrived at a ready formula to meet every problem of life" (*CUFE*, p. 28). Razumov struggled unavailingly to attain such a *modus vivendi* and to reject such "side influences": Conrad, as we have seen, saw no possibility of attaining such a "coherent personality" in post-insurrectionist Poland.

[26] 17 Feb. 1908, MS POSK (Polish Cultural Center, London). Conrad was recovering from another attack of gout.

[27] Conrad, in the spring of 1910, cut only about one thousand words from Part First of the novel, amongst them, three of the biggest sequences treated the generative impulses behind Razumov's record. He was determined to remain behind "the

veil"! He told Galsworthy that he cut "about 30,000 words" from the TS (15 Oct. 1911, *LL*, II:134). See David Leon Higdon's essay for further details.

[28] "Razumov," pp. 284–85, TS, p. 140.

[29] "Razumov," pp. 312–16, TS, pp. 154–55. Incidentally, the narrator's reference to "my personal contact with Mr Razumov drawing near" (written mid-March, 1908) indicates that Conrad still intended to follow the plan outlined to Galsworthy on 6 January. In September/October 1908, when "the clean copy" was prepared, Conrad failed to see how inappropriate the narrator's anticipation had become — Razumov does not reappear until Part Second, Chapter IV.

[30] 2 Sept. 1911, *LL*, II:116. Szittya, "Metafiction: The Double Narration in *Under Western Eyes*," argues that "the hero's duplicity, his doubleness, is a paradigm of the author's" (p. 824) and that "the energies that characterize the novel characterize the man; the aesthetic double structure . . . is an image and a product of a doubleness in Conrad's life and mind" (p. 835). Szitta is reluctant to conclude that *UWE* is "a personal record," but he claims (as I do) that it is "a faithful mirror of Conrad's very real personal conflicts" (p. 837).

[31] 6 Feb. 1910. Jessie remembers that "He spoke all the time in Polish . . . . More than once I opened my eyes to find him tottering towards me in search of something he had dreamed of." In *Joseph Conrad and His Circle* (New York: Dutton, 1935, pp. 143–144).

[32] 3 Nov. 1908 to H. G. Wells, unpublished. My thanks to Laurence Davies, one of the editors of the forthcoming fourth volume of *CL*, for permission to quote.

[33] Preface to *The Nigger of the "Narcissus."*

[34] The suggestive differences and the compelling interrelationships between Conrad's novel and his autobiography deserve a major study. *A Personal Record* claims to be "An exact and imaginative rendering of authentic memories" and is steeped in a Virgilian "spirit of piety" towards all the "emotions" and memories of a "man reviewing his own experience" (p. 25). This "piety" however, together with his conscious determination to

discover a continuity and consistency in his three lives as a Pole, a mariner in the British Merchant Service, and an English novelist ensure that his "personal record" is suffused with personal myth. Cf. Najder's "Introduction" to *The Mirror of the Sea* and *A Personal Record* (Oxford: The World Classics, 1988.) *Under Western Eyes*, as the cancelled MS passages especially suggest, is an alternative, altogether darker, more private version of Conrad's troubled "discourse" with his Polish "shades" than "the public smiling" pages of *A Personal Record*. Cf. Edward Said's *Joseph Conrad and the Fiction of Autobiography* (Cambridge, MA: Harvard U.P., 1966), which analyzes in detail Conrad's attempt to constuct a public persona — one markedly at odds with the figure I depict, who shares many of his personal and writerly problems with Razumov.) The main psychological imperative behind Conrad's decision, in the late summer of 1908, to break off the composition of "Razumov" — when the protagonist was about to reenter the Geneva narrative and therefore confront Natalia — was, probably, his need to write a more cheerful version of Razumov's entrapment and haunting. Moreover his belated recognition of the "tragic significance" of his parents' lives in the first "Reminiscence" spurred, I think, a major reevaluation of "the tragic significance" of the lives of the young Russians in his novel — a reevaluation most evident in the narrator's new found "piety" and compassion, and in the pejorative depiction of Geneva. Similarly, with Razumov poised to confess and about to be deafened, Conrad broke off the composition of Razumov in early December 1909 to write "The Secret Sharer," which is a more hopeful version of Haldin's corrosive sharing of Razumov's life .

[35] Aaron Fogel, *Coercion to Speak: Conrad's Poetics of Dialogue* (Cambridge, MA: Harvard University Press, 1985), p. 211.

[36] 6 Jan. 1908, *LL*, II:65. In the same letter to Galsworthy, Conrad admitted he owed Pinker £1,572. Conrad's biographers have failed to take in the sheer scale of his debts. To convert the sum to modern prices we need, according to Bank of England calculations, to multiply by sixty. Thus Conrad owed his long-

suffering agent the equivalent of £94,320, some $150,000. This sum mounted to about $230,000 by the time he finished the novel two years later — and promptly broke down! Najder in *JCC* is sound on the details of Conrad's debts.

[37] Both phrases are Bobrowski's (*CPB*, pp. 153–54). Milosz concurs with Bobrowski's judgement when he argues that "Korzeniowski's psychology shows that a refusal to accept existence in general was the motivating force behind his actions" (*Mosaic*, 6:4 [1973], 129). Conrad's assessment of his father in a letter to Edward Garnett — "A man of great sensibilities: of exalted and gloomy temperament . . . withal of strong religious feeling degenerating after the loss of his wife into mysticism touched with despair" (*CL*, II:247) — is even more strongly suggestive of Haldin in the MS than in the novel itself. In the holograph Natalia reflects that her brother's assassination of De P— may not have been inspired, "Perhaps he was afraid of despair." The old English teacher in response "pondered for a while and saw . . . . . In those few words there was contained the definition of a character and the philosophy of an action . . . . Not despair but the fear of despair may drive a weak character to desperate action. Or perhaps an earnest character. Levity is the enemy of despair too. Or a man of deep feeling — a shallow nature would not be moved by the apprehension of the supreme danger which lies in despair" ("Razumov," pp. 515–16). It's a pity Conrad cut this wonderful and timely meditation on the psychology of the terrorist; perhaps the passage reminded him too acutely of his father's "deep feeling " and "despair." See Carabine, "From *Razumov* to *Under Western Eyes*: The Dwindling of Natalia Haldin's 'Possibilities,' " *The Ugo Mursia Memorial Lectures*, ed. Mario Curreli, (Milano: Mursia International, 1988), pp. 147–171.

[38] "Autocracy and War"(1905), *Notes on Life and Letters* (Garden City, NY: Doubleday, Page and Co., 1924), p. 102. Compare also "The Crime of Partition"(1919) where Conrad repeats the highly colored claims of the Polish Romantic Nationalists that (say) the Old Polish Commonwealth "offers a singular instance of an extremely liberal administrative federal-

ism which, in its Parliamentary life as well as its international politics, presented a complete unity of feeling and purpose," and which "Even after Poland lost its independence" survived in "all the national movements towards liberation . . . initiated in the name of the whole mass of people inhabiting the limits of the Old Republic, and all the Provinces took part in them with complete devotion" (p. 161). The latter claim, especially dear to Korzeniowski's heart, testifies to the power of a faith to blind one to reality, as Conrad's sardonic depiction of Ziemianitch attests. (Compare also his wry description of the Ukrainian serfs' sacking of his Uncle's, Nicholas B—'s manor house in *A Personal Record* — a sad misfortune for one who fought "pro Patria!" [pp. 57 ff.]). The *szlachta* (the Polish, Catholic gentry) constituted only 10% of the multi-ethnic, multi-religious and multi-lingual population of the Ukraine where Conrad was born. Thus they were divided from the Ukrainian Uniate Christian serfs by race, religion, class and language. Nonetheless Korzeniowski, like many Romantic Nationalists, confidently expected these same serfs to identify their thirst for freedom with their masters' struggle to restore the boundaries of the Old Polish Commonwealth and to oust Muscovite barbarism. They didn't, with disastrous consequences for the 1863 Insurrection. Bobrowski recognized that "our claim that we have a higher culture and a longer history [than the Russians] could be criticized as "only the life and culture of one class" (*CPB*, p. 80). See also Gustav Morf, *The Polish Shades and Ghosts of Joseph Conrad*, (New York: Astra Books, 1976), pp. 26 ff.

[39] "Poland Revisited" (1915), *Notes on Life and Letters*, p. 168.

[40] "Autocracy and War," *Notes on Life and Letters*, p. 98. Aniela Zagorska's conclusion ("I am certain that his hatred towards Russia was kept alive by the constant torment that stemmed from his sense — right or wrong — of guilt in respect of Poland.") is irresistible (*Ibid.*, p. 219).

[41] Following "whom I betrayed most basely," the holograph reads "It was seeing you that I understood this. Most basely.

And therefore perdition is my lot" (p. 1321). Conrad inscribed the changes I discuss, in "batch" "T" of the TS. See Higdon.

[42] This latent "discourse" which surfaces in Conrad's critique of his father's political values and temperament via the presentation of Haldin's ideals and career, countermands the submerged endorsement of his father's onslaught on Russia and helps explain the oft-noted indecisiveness at the heart of the novel — an indecisiveness most plainly evident in the narrator's inconsistent attitudes towards and assessments of Razumov's diary and life, of Haldin's deed, and even, in the negative presentation of Geneva, of Western values and life; and evident also in the ways the novel, especially after part first, begins to question, and on occasion to subvert the old teacher's (and Conrad's?) initial premises.

[43] Conrad borrowed this moving, idealistic description of his mother from Bobrowski's Memoirs (*CUFE*, 25–26).

[44] Freud wrote to Fliess of the "self-reproach that appears regularly among the survivors" (cited in Peter Gay, *Freud: A Life for Our Time* (Garden City, NY: Doubleday–Anchor Books, 1988), p. 88.

[45] "Homo duplex has in my case more than one meaning," 5 Dec. 1903, *CL*, III:89. Conrad's and Razumov's namings are perhaps the most complex in the history of English letters; they combine the conflicts at the heart of their respective cultures and political and historical traditions and of Conrad's vision of life and art: "The only legitimate basis of creative work lies in the courageous recognition of all irreconcilable antagonisms that make our life so enigmatic, so burdensome, so fascinating, so dangerous, so full of hope." (2 Aug. 1901, *CL*, II:348–349). See David Smith's essay in this volume.

The Hidden Narrative: The *K* in Conrad

David R. Smith

"A writer stands confessed in his works."

One of the most striking aspects of Conrad's writing is the intensity of his presence in it, a presence that goes well beyond every writer's need to piece together the observed or experienced as means of achieving a shared reality; and it goes well beyond tricks of style. It is these things, too, but it is much more. His fiction provided him a place where he could live what he had not lived or, more importantly, where he could try to make sense of what he *had* lived, where he could adjust and reform his past to serve the present. This persistent autobiographical current can be seen as deriving in part from his ongoing need to construct an auto-mythology, an undertaking which had both public and private purposes. It was, however, one thing to promote a view of himself as a lonely, romantic sea dog or to convert the attempted suicide's scars on his chest to those of a duellist who had defended a lady's honor, romantic gestures of self-promotion (as, perhaps, though in a rather more radical way, had the attempted suicide itself been); but for a man who valued privacy as much as he did, it was quite another to ponder the deepest sources of his character in the public arena of the novel. It was a behavior self-contradictory, deeply troubling and yet necessary to him. At times it seems almost a game of daring, of now-you-see-it-now-you-don't, but dangerous, for it risked turning the novel into a confessional or a couch. Yet the parallel needs to construct his own myth and public persona and to investigate and recontruct his origins, the sense of his life, were real and led him ambivalently if inexorably into troubled waters. Nowhere are these tendencies more immediate and yet, logically, more ambiguous than in the case of *Under Western Eyes*, the most autobiographical of his novels, the one in which he deals with the matter of his early years. It was the last of his great works and the one toward which *Lord Jim*, "Heart of Darkness," *Nostromo*, *The Secret Agent* had tended.

There are many signs that his personal involvement with this novel troubled him profoundly, from his much discussed "complete nervous breakdown" (*LBM*, 192) upon completing the manuscript to the anxieties evident in the teasing contradictions of his various remarks at the time on the subject of autobiography and the novel. In one of his "Reminiscences" written during a painful and self-reflective hiatus in the composition of *Under Western Eyes* and with that work obviously in mind, Conrad avowed that "a writer of imaginative prose (even more than any other sort of artist) stands confessed in his works. His conscience, his deeper sense of things, lawful and unlawful, gives him his attitude before the world"(*APR*, 95).[1] But the confessional is secret, even secretive, and here, in any event, Conrad only confessed that he confessed and displaced even that admission from one work to another. It was very nearly *un jeu de passe passe*. Feeling as he did the dangers of self-revelation, he was as actively engaged in concealing, in protecting, as in confessing a "conscience

. . . lawful and unlawful." As he wrote to a friend on 13 May 1909, more or less as he finished with *Some Reminiscences* and once again took up *Under Western Eyes*: "I lay my temperament quite bare before the world in the assurance that the world at large will never perceive the whole extent of my sincerity."[2] Though his apparent assurance arose from an assumption that the reader would not know enough to recognize the truth of his confession, he took care in the evolving process of revision to hide much of what he had earlier revealed. As he later (in September 1911) wrote in "A Familiar Preface" to *A Personal Record* (a "Preface" intended "to explain (in a sense) how I came to write such a novel"),[3] even though "a novelist .... is only writing about himself .... the disclosure is not complete" (xii).

This sense of teasing confession, of incomplete disclosure, the reader's uncanny knowledge that there is something more and deeper in his works than is revealed, is a central element in Conrad's voice. But in *Under Western Eyes*, the novel in which he most frequently sought "discourse with the shades" of his past, the covert confession is more than a matter of voice: it becomes in some sort a subterranean narrative, one which can be at least partially excavated by turning to the privacy of "Razumov," its manuscript, where the confession is more complete. There, before he had begun the process of hedging his disclosures, we see more clearly the intimacy and nature of his engagement.

Conrad in His Manuscripts

His manuscripts are extraordinary resources, offering clues to the creative history of much of his work. *Almayer's Folly*, for instance, having traveled over half the globe with him, shows signs of the voyaging: on a verso which he took to Poland with him on his 1890 visit, we find him playing with his name, his identity, a matter that surely loomed large amidst admonitions about his heritage, about what he had to live up to and to live down. In bold, hand-printed Gothic black letter, he spelled out what was for him his genetic self, "Konrad."[4]

He was often preoccupied with the semiotics of his identity, an absorption that has been noted by readers from Richard Curle, who remarked Conrad's habit of jotting his initials in books, to Professors Karl and Najder, who comment on the different signatures Conrad used, signings which seem to represent roughly the three lives: Polish, maritime and/or legal British, and authorial.[5] These signatures (and their initials) are varied and chosen to suit the occasion, but schematically put, they were *Konrad Korzeniowski* or *K.K.*, *Joseph Conrad Korzeniowski* or *J.C.K.*, and *Joseph Conrad* or *J.C.* There is obvious layering in these identities, though *Konrad Korzeniowski* or *K.K.*, or more simply, *Konrad,* or still more simply, *K,* was the deepest. Konrad is what he was because it is what he was called (Konrad or Konradek at home as a child), and it was the *K* in Konrad which, having been Anglicized to a *C,* became a refuge from change, from alternative personas, from the contingent.

He played with these signs, impersonated himself. For example, in January 1894, the second mate, Joseph Conrad Korzeniowski, already deeply engaged in writing *Almayer's Folly* and unknowingly leaving the sea for good, or so the myth has it, signed off the *Adowa* as "J. Conrad,"[6] a close approximation of the English authorial identity given him somewhat later at T. Fisher Unwin's, again according to the legend, but already assumed here. Then, in the spring of 1894, discouraged because he had not heard from Unwin, he retreated from the English *J. Conrad* persona and suggested to Marguerite Poradowska that the novel should be translated and published as their joint work: "The name 'Kamoudi' in small print somewhere will do. Let your name appear on the title page — an explanatory note saying that K. collaborated will be enough. Will you agree?"[7]

If he jotted these signs in books and used them to arrange his fantasy life, it is not surprising that he put them in those manuscripts that involve a deep sense of himself: *Lord Jim, Nostromo, Under Western Eyes.* On a verso of the *Lord Jim* manuscript, he jotted, "Konrad." Elsewhere he wrote that on board they kept "Calashee" watch, then corrected the spelling by writing a *K* over the *C*, the shift from *C* to *K* nudging him into a reverie. In the margin he jotted a column of three *K*'s.

The psychological siting of *Nostromo*, though deeply personal to Conrad, is more of this world, less internalized than *Lord Jim*, and its marginal musings take a different turn. *Jim* is seen from the inside out, tragically, *Nostromo* from the outside, panoramically, though Decoud's suicide and its explanations surely forced him to open windows within himself and though much of the rest of the novel rose out of what he had witnessed and suffered as a child of the devastation of love and family by politics. But despite his personal experience of what he describes, rather than imaginatively reentering it, he distances himself from it and uses it in a way that is determined in part by the externalizing imperatives of history, politics, and economics. It is a manner enabled by his having achieved a public platform in a British-centered western European world. It is not surprising then that on several pages of the manuscript he drew a number of carefully elaborated monograms using his British initials *J.C.K.* and in lesser number, *J.C.*

"Razumov," the Manuscript

Then what of *Under Western Eyes*, this most auto-biographical novel that shook his emotions so fundamentally as after its completion to cause a psychotic episode in which, for a startling two weeks, he hallucinated and "held converse" in Polish with his characters (*LBM*, 192)? Not surprisingly, at least seen in this light, the manuscript abounds in marginal *K*'s, as does no other, six dozen of them, a few superimposed with an *R*, signs of a deep personal involvement with the story, an identification with the hero, Razumov. If they are, we need to see where and under what circumstances they occur (and, conversely, where they do not) in order to understand them.

He did not jot them in all the places one might expect. For example, in Part First, they occur only at page 204 even though all of this first part (through 339)[8] seems rather obviously autobiographically encoded: Conrad orphans Razumov, gives him a phantom father who is identified only as "Prince K—." Insisting on the distinction between the Eastern *K* and the Western *C*, he first introduces us to his protagonist as, "Cyril son of Isidor — Kyrilo Sidorovitch — Razumov." Razumov, like Dostoevsky's Razumihin, takes his name from a root which suggests the mind, reason, whereas Kyrilo is utterly Slav, the name that of St. Cyril, author of the Cyrillic alphabet, so that Razumov is *homo duplex* even in name, as was Conrad whose *nom de plume* was divided between the prudent half of his family tree (his first name was taken from Józef Bobrowski, his maternal grandfather) and the fiery nationalist half (Konrad was taken from Konrad Wallenrod, hero of the Polish epic). Moreover, not only is each split between conceptions of rational accomodation and patriotic passion, each is divided between East and West. Razumov is described as having an

English manner, and Conrad regarded himself as both Polish and English. Moreover, Razumov is a borrowed name, as was Joseph Conrad, for it is not his family name. Indeed, his first name, Kyrilo, and his father's name, Prince K—, are together suggestive of links to Konrad Korzeniowski, Conrad's usual Polish identity. And as it was with Conrad, Razumov, this "young man of no parentage," was forced to quit his "corner of the world" (11, 32), to leave an identity that, though tenuous and assaulted,[9] was his, for a footing and identity that were contingent, doubtful, and fragile because of the intrusive and devastating effects of someone else's radical political theory upon his history and continuity. The difference between them is, of course, fundamental. In Razumov's case the intruder was a fellow student, whereas in Conrad's it was his father. Part First is, in effect, Conrad's disguised *apologia*, yet there are no *K*'s except for the isolated instance at 204, which, in a sense, gives it added weight.

Where then do the *K*'s occur? First, only when the narration permits Razumov to be at the center of the action, which facilitates Conrad's identification with him. When the narrator takes over, Conrad distances himself from his protagonist, and the *K*'s stop. Second, with the exception of the one incidence at page 204, they occur only in the last third of a manuscript of 1351 sheets, appearing between pages 861 and 1314, most particularly between 1024 and 1314, with a hiatus from 1183 to 1246 during which the narrator is at the center. These manuscript pages include the following passages: Razumov's meeting with Peter Ivanovitch and his Egeria of the painted face at the Chateau Borel (though there are only a few *K*'s), the long conversation between Razumov and Sophia Antonovna (1024–1102), the conversation between Razumov and Julius Laspara, including the ruminations afterward (1103–1123) (these two form the last third of Part 3), the flashback to Petersburg (1124–1182 — the first quarter of Part 4), and Razumov's conversation with Mrs. Haldin and confession to Natalia, (1247– 1314 — the third quarter of Part 4). This is work written during the last five months of 1909.[10]

To understand the occurrence of the *K*'s and their connections with the text, one must know something of the history of its composition, the overriding fact of which is that it was written in a tangle of high tensions and low depressions. He was deeply in debt, his books were not selling well, he had no income except that which he borrowed from Galsworthy or was advanced by Pinker, he had to beg and borrow to take care of Borys's schooling, and both he and Jesse had health problems. In addition, as the writing advanced, Conrad became painfully involved with his story in a confessional, self-analytical way, present miseries engaging the memory of past griefs.

Despite his problems, the first stage of the writing, comprising all of Part First (December 1907 to mid-March 1908 [1–139]), went well, surely because he had thought it through before starting. The second stage (mid-March to 13 October 1908 [339–668]), however, developed problems. For one, the scene shifts from Petersburg to Geneva, and in context that meant that Razumov's diary was no longer sufficient as the basis of narration. The ineffectual language teacher, who heretofore had simply presented the diary, now had to be made into a credible character. For another, Natalia Haldin and her mother entered the story at this point and presented Conrad with the problem women characters had always given him. For still another, Conrad's conception of the plot was changing. It was to have been a short story with a formulaic twist: Razumov marries Natalia, who gives him a child. The child looks so much like Haldin that Razumov, guilt-ridden, confesses. The second stage then would have been the last; but as it began to develop in Conrad's mind, he gave up the mechanical ending and began to probe Razumov's psyche and moral condition. Mikulin's question at the end of Part First ("Where to?") became a challenge to the author even more than to the character.

In its third stage (14 October 1908 to 28 July 1909 [666–898]), the writing grew more difficult as it dealt with the problems created by a changing story. A major complication here was Razumov's reentry onto the scene, a problem complicated by the fact that he became a less self-justifying and sinned-against version of Conrad and instead turned into a deliberate transgressor (little wonder that Conrad was preoccupied with the lawful and unlawful aspects of self-confession and the novel). And as that was happening in his fiction, he began to avoid "Razumov" by joining Hueffer in the hectic intimacy of founding the *English Review* and then, at Hueffer's suggestion, by starting on his reminiscences. These reminiscences were closely linked to the matter of *Under Western Eyes*, but because the manner of dealing with them was more objective and externalized, it was easier for him to stay on the surface, to make the deeper truths suitable for daylight, and it offered him an escape from the torment Razumov was causing him. The reminiscences took precedence and became a means of avoiding "Razumov," which he worked at intermittently and ineffectually. He became more and more evasive, defensive, less honest, increasingly involved in an unfortunately transparent confidence game with Pinker. Pinker, who had been bankrolling Conrad and who needed a completed novel, was intensely displeased and intensified his pressure on Conrad.

During the first half of 1909 Conrad's difficulties became intolerable. Added to all his other insecurities, he felt that his place in literature was being denied him. He knew that he should be able to make a claim as a major English novelist, and it galled him that he was regarded by some as a kind of curiosity. He was furious about a dreadful, Toryishly nationalistic review of *A Set of Six* in the *Daily News* which pretended that as he was not British born and bred, his English could not be as it ought and recommended that he write in Polish and have it translated.[11] Garnett continued to claim that there was a Slavic quality in his work, and became an irritant. He felt assaulted by British obtuseness and tactlessness. And yet, if they used his Polish birth as an escape from understanding his work, he remembered Poles who didn't understand him either. He was damned either way.

His despair deepened in the spring and early summer, hitting bottom at the end of July. In March the Conrads had moved from Someries back to Kent, to quarters that Hueffer had located for them in Aldington so that they could work together — four rooms over a butcher's shop which smelled of curing room and abattoir and resounded on "killing days" with the squeals of pigs being slaughtered.[12] The quarters were so cramped that the only place he could find to work was a windowless cubicle. It was a "hole," he wrote Galsworthy at the end of July, and was "growing more odious" every day.[13] Not long after arriving there, he came down with a severe influenza followed by an equally severe depression which provided a perfect matrix for the crises yet to come during the summer.

Though he had turned to Hueffer in the last months of 1908, Hueffer had always presented something of a problem to the Conrad household. Conrad's own reactions to him were changeable, and Jesse disliked him, responses that were sorely worked upon during this period. When without warning on Easter Sunday 1909 Hueffer invited himself, Elsie, and Conrad's physician, Robert D. Mackintosh, to dinner at the Conrads, Conrad joined with Jesse in turning them away, which left him the task of explaining to Mackintosh that though the latter was always welcome, he had had to take a stand against Hueffer's "mania for managing the universe, worse even in form than in substance."[14] A few weeks later Hueffer wrote an insolent letter to Conrad, accusing him of having refused to receive Willa Cather. On 20 May Conrad answered: "Stop this nonsense with me Ford. It's ugly. I won't have it."[15] By the end of July, Conrad was addressing him not as Ford but as Hueffer, and on the 31st of July he broke off their friendship and his relations with the *English Review*.[16] Moreover, the *English Review* failed financially during this period and was rescued in the autumn by Hueffer's brother-in-law, Dr. David Soskice, a political anarchist, a Russian, and, according to Conrad, a "horrid Jew."[17] He would have nothing more to do with it, though eventually *Under Western Eyes* would be serialized there.

He was at wit's end about his finances — he tried and failed in an attempt to speculate with his life insurance, failed to get another government grant, was £2,250 in debt, nearly all of that with Pinker with whom his difficulties had reached a crisis point, also at the end of July. His 1909 debt translates in 1989 into approximately £135,000 or $216,000.[18] Pinker now began using carrot and stick by proposing to withhold his usual £6 advances if he did not receive regular batches of manuscript. It is a sum which at first glance seems modest, but it converts to a rather substantial £360 or $576. Conrad was outraged ("You need not treat me as a journeyman joiner.")[19] and foolish in his injured pride. He had earlier threatened to write the rest of the novel in French and now threatened to hurl the manuscript into the fire.[20] His anguish would affect the fourth stage by drawing him ever more intimately into his novel, causing him to identify with it still more closely, a reversible equation, for his deepening engagement with Razumov surely caused him greater anguish. A sprinkling of *K*'s begins in the last pages of stage three.

But it is in the fourth stage (from 28 July 1909 to 22 January 1910 [898–1351]), most particularly from 1024 through 1314, in work done between the end of September and late December, that most of the *K*'s occur. The accumulating problems from the spring and summer turned his writing into a painful retreat into his formative past, into a communion with his beginnings; and it is at that point that the marginal *K*'s appear in number. They stop as suddenly following 1314 during the confession to Natalia. The writing from there to 1321 flounders badly in the manuscript; it seems aimless, adrift, and was almost entirely deleted, which, along with the sudden cessation of the *K*'s, suggests this as a point at which he momentarily stopped work on "Razumov." Exact dating of most passages is difficult to determine because of the way he worked at different tasks more or less simultaneously, so that on any given stretch of writing, he might be occupied with several sections of "Razumov" as well as with finishing or correcting "The Secret Sharer." Whatever the exact synchronicities, he was struggling with Natalia Haldin and her mother at about the time he wrote "The Secret Sharer," which gives his note to Garnett regarding that story ("No damned tricks with girls there. Eh?") particular meaning (*LG*, 243).[21]

"The Secret Sharer" put him in much better spirits, and after finishing it he went back to work on the final stretch of "Razumov," dating the last page of the manuscript, 22 January 1910. It went well. Once he had got by the confession to Natalia, the rest was foreordained — public confession, punishment, atonement, and reincorporation. He wrote it quickly and purposefully — there are relatively few corrections in the manuscript, most of them occurring in the typescript, the contrary of a usually fairly labored manuscript and relatively clean typescript, in which alterations are ordinarily simple deletions. The major changes occurred in a rewriting in holograph of the last thirty-seven pages done between the 22nd and the 26th of January.[22] He refined the writing either in the typescript or, as with the ending, by a complete revision. In other words, he was clear about the general direction. Even the changes he made consisted of forceful rewrites rather than messy corrections. He was anxious to get on, to finish, and wrote quickly. The challenge to the inner man was no longer the same, and this work contains no *K*'s.

As we look into the *K*'d passages we can see that they occur in those portions that reflect two different areas of distress, the anguish of his current life and that produced by his probing more profoundly into the past and the central issue in his life — the conflicting claims made upon him by what his father and his uncle represented personally and ideologically. It is little wonder, then, that, with *Under Western Eyes* in mind, he warned his reader, "the disclosure is not complete" (*APR*, xiii). His confessions may not be full (these are not, after all, legal depositions), but the *K*'s are emotional responses that indicate imaginative links — sympathies of mood, recognition of parallels, secret confessions to self — between Conrad and his text, and that is how they should be read.

Present Sorrows

Razumov's encounter with Julius Laspara differs somewhat from the rest of this part of the novel in several respects. It is less organically necessary than those with Sophia or Natalia or the flashback to Petersburg, and the narrative tone differs. Until we come to Razumov's reactions at the end of it, the manuscript version has a comic edge (albeit savagely so, as in his description of Laspara's grandson) not found elsewhere. And the passages he has marked reflect not only the dichotomies of his past but the sorrows of his present, for the *K*'s indicate an unexpected subtext which rises out of Conrad's immediate surroundings — out of the windowless cubicle in Aldington, found for him by Hueffer, where he was spilling himself onto paper and hoping that he was adequate. He is in unsatisfactory quarters because Hueffer didn't find him better and because he has little money. He has little money because Pinker won't advance him large sums and because his novels don't sell well — perhaps because he has a Slavic mentality. And he can't seem to finish what he's working on, can't seem to write, can't even find a place to write, and, therefore, can't satisfy all the demands being made on him. It is a mocking despair that enters the novel in this passage. Here, through Laspara, Conrad is able to strike out against those he perceived as bedevilling him, and, indeed, against his own failings.

Behind the screen of Razumov's loathing for Laspara is Conrad responding to an agent demanding copy and withholding advances, to a Germanizing, philandering, know-it-all and pushy editor, to an anarchist Russian emigré, perhaps even to an old friend who finds him too Slavic, and above all else, to his own despair. It is a world badgering Conrad and bringing him near the breaking point; and it is this world that appears to have inspired the dozen *K*'s in these few pages.

Laspara first greets Razumov in German ("And how is Herr Razumov?") which "alone made him more odious."[23] Conrad jots a *K* on the bottom left of page 1103, where he writes that Laspara is a:

Polyglot, of unknown parentage, of indefinite nationality,

anarchist with a pedantic and ferocious temperament and an amazingly inflammatory turn for invective . . . . [nearly matched here by Conrad] For the rest he lived in the upper [there is a *K* in the margin] town in an old sombre narrow house left him by some naive middle-class admirer of his humanitarian eloquence.

Laspara has two daughters, one of whom has a pasty-faced son of six. One cannot tell which of the two is the mother. Laspara knows, of course, though he does not know who the father is; "but with admirable pedantry he had refrained from asking her for details, no, not so much as the name of the father because maternity [there is an obliterated *K* in the margin] should be an anarchist function" (1105). This casual view of marriage and family was obviously more than the orphaned Conrad could handle, particularly at this point in his life when he had to ask for help in supporting his own family. Lurking behind this group portrait is, amongst others, Hueffer, whose family life was in ruins, who had deserted his wife and two daughters and who, anarchically, was having affairs with two women at the same time; and standing a little further behind was Hueffer's brother-in-law David Soskice, of anarchist persuasion, and surely a polyglot.

Making an effort at amiability, Laspara addresses Razumov in Russian, which "he spoke, as he spoke and wrote four or five other European languages, without distinction and without force other than that of sustained invective." There is a *K* centered at the bottom of this page (1107). Here is more than contempt for a linguistically clumsy polyglot. It is also a means of differentiating himself as stylist from the charge of being a Slavic curiosity somehow able to write English, as the reviewer for the *Daily News* seemed to think he was. Laspara urges Razumov to write, which occasions a *K*. In a response which recalls his

rage over slurs about his English and about his Slavic qualities as an author, Conrad wrote, (he began the line with
a *K*) "Razumov muttered rather surlily that he did not
even know English." Laspara, sounding like the reviewer
for the *Daily News*, answers, "Write in Russian. We'll have
it translated"(1109).

A major aspect of the subtext in this passage (and it is
what it has been leading to) is writing, for Hueffer, Pinker,
Soskice, and Garnett (further in the background), who so
exercised him, were, one way or another, involved in his
writing, as, of course, his own father was. Virtually every
use of the word "write" triggers a *K*. Laspara expects Razumov (unbeknownst to him an anti-revolutionary) to write
about revolution, but the latter is momentarily blocked
by the confusions of his situation which will lead him to
an eventual confession urged upon him by moral rather
than ideological imperatives. Razumov mirrors the anti-
revolutionary Conrad, whose writing is blocked in part because he was dealing with the tug of rival positions whose
daylight appearance was ideological and easy to adjudicate,
but whose deeper and darker causes arose from the wrench-
ing competition of divided loyalties, that is to say, from his
most profound moral commitments. Much of this novel engaged him in a confrontation with the repudiations fidelity
requires.

Laspara also served Conrad to satirize some of Hueffer's views about writing, or Conrad's version of them, for
Laspara "could not understand how any one could refrain
from writing on anything, social, economic, historical —
anything." In fact, Laspara has a friend in London who has
been in touch with a review of advanced ideas surely the
(*English Review*).

After Laspara had left him, Razumov "spat violently,
.... 'Cursed Jew!' .... Julius Laspara might have been a

Transylvanian, a Turk, an Andalusian, or a citizen of one of the Hanse towns for anything he could tell to the contrary. But this is not a story [*K* crossed out] of the West, and this exclamation must be recorded, accompanied by the comment that it was merely an expression of [*K*] hate and contempt" (1110). Is Conrad attenuating the violent phrase he used to Galsworthy about Soskice? Razumov walks away, "his eyes fixed on the ground .... The insistence of the celebrated subversive journalist rankled in his mind strangely. Write. Must write! He! Write! A sudden light flashed upon him. To write was the very thing he had made up his mind to do that day." There is a vertical string of *K*'s alongside this passage. Again there seem to be two referants, for the writing Razumov is remembering is his spy report, which is a further deliberate betrayal, but strangely *duplex* in the circumstance since he is also about to write his confession; but the writing Conrad is thinking about is his manuscript and the problems Razumov's duplexities are causing him. It is a strange rankling, indeed.

One can feel Conrad's own pain in Razumov. " 'Indeed! I shall write — never fear. Certainly. That's why I am here. And for the future I shall have something to write about.' He was exciting himself by this mental soliloquy" (1112). Conrad seems to be responding to his own writing difficulties and to the detested pressures being brought to bear upon him to turn out copy. He continues, "But the idea of writing evoked the thought of a place to write, of shelter, of privacy and naturally of his lodgings." There are two *K*'s in margin and two more at bottom of page. The passage brings us abruptly back to Aldington and the windowless cubicle in four rooms over a butcher's shop rented for him by Hueffer. It brings us back to what must have been his state of mind — his high ideals as an artist, misunderstood by some, and from that to his feelings of self-pity and anger over his obligation to grind out a novel which was painfully, revealingly personal, to pour the inner man onto the page while being treated as a kind of cottage industry, a manufactory of fictional product, by a businessman agent, and as a curiosity by some English critics who, of course, did not know the half of it.

Homo Duplex

There are common denominators in these passages, including the dialogue with Julius Laspara, that rise out of his past, for either they deal with betrayal and guilt or are sardonic renderings of political attitudes that particularly affected Razumov/Conrad and moved him to contempt, another face of remorse.[24] There is in them a moral progression that moves away from Razumov's largely untried convictions (and the desperate and nearly reflexive self-defense) of Part First to test them through willed action. Belief thus probed produces remorse, anagnorisis, expiation and reincorporation. The *K*'s are attached to passages that move from fear of exposure and something between pity and contempt for the true revolutionary (Sophia Antonovna), to disgust with the tainted opportunism of the not so true (Laspara and briefly Peter Ivanovitch and Necator), to, retrospectively, complicity in the guilt, followed by self-accusation (in the flashback to Petersburg), to confession (Natalia).

The flashback that opens Part Four and is the continuation of Part First, returns the novel to the East, to origins. The scenes in Geneva tend to deal with guilt as it manifests itself in Razumov's conduct, whether he is defending himself, wrestling with his conscience, or confessing his sins; but in Petersburg Conrad develops the growing complexity of Razumov's guilt as Councillor Mikulin converts the betrayer into a spy and in so doing takes from him the mantle of victim, of being sinned against. In the margins of passages exposing this growing sense of his participation and complicity in the creation of his own fate *K*'s abound.

At the end of Part First, Razumov, self-defensively trying to remain aloof, declares to Mikulin that he shall take the liberty to retire. Mikulin holds him with the question, "Where to?" He cannot answer because within the autocracy the choice is not his. But Mikulin is friendly, reminds him of his "interesting piece of paper," his articles of faith, the responses of an orphan who desperately wants to belong, and draws him in with the "murmur of abstract ideas." "This conversation (and others later on) . . . [*K*] brought Mr. Razumov as we know him to the test of another faith"(1127). Razumov tries to defend his detachment, but Mikulin will have none of it. "I understand your liberalism," he says. "I have an intellect of that kind myself. Reform for me is mainly a question of method. But the principle of revolt is a physical intoxication, a sort of hysteria which must be kept away from the masses. You agree — don't you?" "Well then there must not be anything equivocal in such an assent. There is [elaborate *K* with a *C* imposed] danger to the state in the reserves of some individual minds and we are here to look to that"(1128). "[*K*] Mr Razumov listening with a faint smile wondered whether this was not something in the nature of an unoffical warning. His position had made him [*K*] suspicious and very sensitive. But [*K*] suppressing his exasperation he asked Councillor Mikulin point blank if that meant he was going to have him watched. [para.] The high official took no [*K*] offense at the cynically careless tone"1129).

Despite his wary reactions, Razumov comes to accept Mikulin's point of view, though without apparent conviction, because Mikulin's arguments, having the reality of authority and of the status quo, are comfortable. Razumov has been searching for a formula of peace, and his acceptance finds its correlative in his response to the dreaded police headquarters: the "big room in [*K*] the heart, as it were, of the police office seemed a peaceful refuge infinitely removed from the work of strife"(1131). However, Razumov's (and Conrad's) ambivalences are still at work, for at the bottom of the page there are a pair of *K*'s under the phrase, "A great disquiet made his heart beat quicker," which echoes the "ponderous blow" his "leaden heart" struck as he betrayed Haldin (204).

What are Conrad's connections with these "imagined things, happenings, people," this "invented world?" Though, as he asserts, he may be "writing about himself" and discoursing "with the shades"(*APR*, xiii), it is not a simple algebra of symbols that he has created. It is rather in the psychological reverberations, the highly imaginative projections and parallel fantasies that one recognizes the kinship between Razumov and Conrad. As a child he was self-conscious, sensitive and in all probability suspicious as he moved from one household, one set of rules and rulers to another. He found adult authority difficult and had problems of manner when dealing with his superiors: his grandmother/guardian gave up on him; he was forced to leave an orphanage for having presumed to court the director's daughter and for insubordination.[25] Above all, he was torn between mixed memories of his patriot father, for whom the "principle of revolt" may well have been "a physical intoxication, a sort of hysteria," and the training of his meliorist uncle/guardian, who tried to bring him to a prudent acceptance of the status quo so that he could work within it. His youth, particularly after his father's death, was, in some respects, a rebellious young man's education in right reason, which is to say, given his ambivalences, in duplicity. He was, as he describes Razumov, an "uncommon young man . . . with his peculiar temperament, his unsettled mind and shaken conscience, struggling in the toils of a false position"(1166).

At the start of Part Four, in a passage which is followed by a *K* (1124), we are asked to pity poor Razumov because he is alone in the world, a view not unlike that in Part First; but as Part Four develops, the moral dimensions of the story take on a new complexity as do Conrad's ties to it. Razumov's betrayal of Haldin had occurred in the confusion and pressure of the moment, though it was, of course, self-serving; but he became a spy deliberately, and having accepted the assignment, threw himself into it, even adding his own touches to further the revolutionaries' delusions, "which credited him with a mysterious share in the Haldin affair." He comes upon a student acquaintance, friendly and foolish Kostia, and uses him to prepare the final touches of his departure. He induces Kostia (I hesitate to remark that his name begins with a *K*) to steal from his father for him.

Here, at the point where Razumov has fully agreed to spy, to transgress deliberately, Conrad appears to make a secret confession of deliberate transgressions of his own. The scene has a familiar feel, for it is reminiscent of Conrad's financial abuses of his dear old uncle Bobrowski, abuses which on one occasion rose out of his spending his year's allowance in a brief period and then attempting suicide, which had the effect of getting his uncle to come to Marseille to settle his debts (to get money to give Razumov Kostia must steal from his father because he has just spent his entire allowance) and on another consisted in his elaborately faking participation in a shipwreck so as to pry money out of him.[26] When Razumov pushes him to the act, Kostia says, "He will be terribly upset, but, you know, the dear old duffer really loves me"(1181). The phrase cut so close to the bone that in the typescript Conrad repeated it: "You see the dear old duffer really loves me. He'll be hurt." On the next page (1182) Kostia goes off to break into his father's desk crying:[27]

> 'To the devil with the ten comman-
> dements! [sic]' cried the other. *This is*
> *the new future now.'*
> with [the] greatest animation. 'It's
> the new future now.'
> K But when he entered Razumov's
> room late in the evening it was
> with an unaccustomed soberness
> of manner, almost solemnly.
> K 'It's done,' he said.
> Razumov sitting bowed, his
> clasped hands hanging between his knees
> shuddered at the sound of these
> words. The other *laid on the*
> deposited [slowly in the circle of lamplight] *on the table*
>   a small
> K brown paper parcel tied with
> a piece of string.

The betrayal and remorse in this passage are marked by the *K*'s and by the expression, "It's done,"[28] which exactly echoes Razumov's self-communion just after Haldin had left his rooms to go out into the night: Razumov begins to tremble, drops his watch, which stops as time ends three minutes short of midnight, and then says to himself, "It's done . . . "(208). The remorse is further born out by the way Conrad disposes of the money; Razumov throws it out the train window because it is trash.

It is an incident that Conrad cannot let alone. Very near the end of the novel, in Razumov's confession to Natalia, he writes, "But make no mistake. Note that my heart is bad. Haven't I induced that poor innocent fool to steal his father's money. He was a fool but not a thief. I made him one." This passage constitutes a confession "unlawful," and the K's signal its importance to Conrad. Kostia and Razumov merge into the K's in the margins as Conrad confesses both his fecklessness and his dishonesty. Conrad seems to be saying, I am both of them: "Note that my heart is bad."

Guilt and Its Sources

How does this novel, which started out as (among other things) somewhat self-pitying and self-justifying (if one accepts these autobiographical implications), turn into (among other things) a confession of guilt and remorse? It is instructive to look back at Part First, so different in tone and intention from what follows, but containing the seeds of the changes that would take place. Though Part First adds a new and openly political dimension to Conrad's ongoing creation of a personal myth, the original short story plot, of which it was a part, is psychologically less complex and less truthful. As the novel progresses and the ambivalences of Razumov's character are exposed, and with them both his guilt and his victimization, the moral situation of the other actors, including the political players, becomes more ambiguous and interesting.

At some level, the Razumov of Part First served Conrad as a means of exculpation from Eliza Orzeskowa's durable charge that he had deserted Poland.[29] It is why Razumov assumes Bobrowski's orderly, meliorist position: he tried his best to get along, but Fate intruded. Conrad had grounds for feeling that circumstances had forced him to leave Poland (though his reasons at the time may not have been entirely clear), and Razumov's plight is a rationalized fantasy, an imaginative reconstitution of the reasons for Conrad's departure, which hardly could be called desertion. However attractive the accusation of national desertion might be to the romantically patriotic, it is a charge arising out of the desires and needs of the accuser; and however compelling the idea of guilt stemming from that putative desertion is to the critic, it is based in a combination of too little information and too much imagination. The origins of Conrad's sense of guilt surely were more fundamental and more complex. On the other hand, that he did not feel that he had betrayed Poland as Orzeskowa would have it did not mean that he did not feel guilt (whose sources were more powerful and intimate and were inextricably tied to Poland and politics), nor did it mean that he did not feel pain and the need to defend his honor. Guilt, whose causes and boundaries are seldom well defined, preoccupied him. And because it was his underlying subject in *Under Western Eyes*, the questions endure: why is it so omnipresent, what is its genesis here?

A hint occurs when Kostia steals from his father, for Tadeusz Bobrowski, became a surrogate father, an affectionate moral center and teacher. His morality was of a conventional, prudent, spend-not-want-not sort — good sense in a dangerous world.[30] He continually assured Conrad that, as he had the wilder Korzeniowski blood in him and with it genetic tendencies toward fecklessness, he needed counsel regarding forethought and prudence. He took good care of Conrad, who returned his affection, who cheated him on more than one occasion, and who felt guilty, as we have just seen confessed. And this remembered guilt was surely reenforced by Conrad's actual financial plight as he wrote, which owed in large part to his deplorable management and lack of the ant-like or beaverish Bobrowski qualities his uncle urged on him. But Conrad's fiction is so guilt filled and he played with that emotion in the margins of this manuscript in such a way as to suggest that his cheating then made Razumov's leaden heart [strike a ponderous blow] ~~flutter within Haldin~~, ley springing up briskly.

"So be it" he cried sadly in a low ~~funeral~~ distinct tone. "Farewell then."

Razumov started forward but ~~even~~ the sight of Haldin's raised hand checked him before he could get away from the table. He leaned on it heavily, listening ~~to hear~~ the faint sounds of some town clock ~~striking~~ tolling the hour. Haldin already at the door tall and straight as an arrow with his pale face and a hand raised ~~waiting~~ attentively ~~poised~~ posed for the statue of a daring youth listening to an ~~voice~~ inner voice. Razumov

Bobrowski only served to prove what he already knew of himself, that his regrets vis à vis Bobrowski can be only a part of the picture. To complete it, we must go back to Part First of "Razumov," to a moment when he was still telling the tale he started to tell.

There, in a story otherwise under control, at manuscript 204, surrounded by other jottings (*S*'s, *Mrs*, and a pair of *K*'s) centered at the top of the page, almost as a title, is a large *K* carefully superimposed with an *R*. This deliberate merging appears at a moment of high tension. Razumov has just returned from his abortive trip to fetch Ziemianitch and after his denunciation of Haldin, who at this point, no longer a phantom in the snow, is quite real.[31] "Struggling in the toils of a false position," (1166) Razumov is nervous and ill-at ease, accuses Haldin, who is a son, a brother, who has a "domestic tradition" and "fireside prejudices," of stripping from him what little *is* his (199). And he attacks Haldin's bloody violence: "what can you people do by scattering a few drops of blood on the snow? On this Immensity. On this unhappy Immensity! I tell you . . . that what . . . [this country] needs is not a lot of haunting phantoms that I could walk through — but a man" (200). Haldin recoils in horror, remains still for a moment, and (204 starts here) "then made Razumov's leaden heart strike a ponderous blow by standing up briskly," [32] for it is the sign that Haldin is going to step out into the death Razumov has prepared for him, and by doing so, ironically, he ceases for the moment to be a phantom and becomes a man. Before and after this moment, Razumov could rationalize his action, could deal with the symbols of his premonitions and fears, but here the effect of his action is electric and inescapable. It is the most personal, concrete moment of Razumov's betrayal and guilt, and at page 204, Conrad has isolated and marked it by putting both their signs upon it.

Conrad could become so involved with, could so join himself to Razumov as he betrayed Haldin only if both betrayer and betrayed had a real grip on Conrad's being. In what one might call a Bobrowskian mode, Conrad clearly identified with Razumov, the meliorist who would get along in society but who was being prevented from doing so by Haldin, a revolutionary theorist, who symbolized what his father represented in politics and character. Here were the two halves of the duality Conrad felt in himself.

Korzeniowski was a populist who believed in the regenerative power of the (non-Polish) peasantry,[33] a position very like Haldin's, for both were romantics in politics, believers in the mystical and healing spirit of the people. He was the moving spirit of a Polish society, "The Trinity," whose patriotic aim was at first a spiritual attempt to "nourish resistance to the idea then insinuating itself into the class from which most of the students came that national emancipation could be achieved through political co-operation with Russia or with the Tsar,"[34] which was essentially Bobrowski's quietist position. "The Trinity" gradually became politicized, creating a network of students from all over Poland and eventually establishing contact with General Mierosławski, an ally of the anarchist Bakunin. Apollo thus became involved with violent anarchists and terrorists. Indeed, one of the charges in the proceedings that led to his exile was that he was the founder of a group known as "Mierosławski's Reds."[35]

Conrad would not admit that his father was a "Red," though from the years of their living in isolation together and from Bobrowski's negative comments, he knew that he was a romantic firebrand. He was caught in a double bind, for the adolescent lessons in conservative politics he received from Bobrowski tended to put the argument genetically, feckless Korzeniowskis on one side, prudent Bobrowskis on the other, conveniently forgetting a number of facts along the way, such as the revolutionary activities of his own brother, a leader of the "Reds." And, despite the facts, by insisting on his sister's (Conrad's mother's) prudent, non-revolutionary, Bobrowska qualities, Bobrowski reenforced in young Conrad's mind Apollo's self-accusations vis à vis his wife's death, a litany that Conrad heard during their exile. Bobrowski used the father, whom he viewed as an irresponsible and dangerous radical dreamer, as an object lesson for the son, an example of what Conrad should not become. It was a political argument that Conrad accepted and at some level found useful, though it meant having to betray his father, to whom he was deeply if ambivalently attached. It also meant having to reject part of himself, as he was often accused by his uncle of favoring the Korzeniowski side of his heritage. His denial that his father was a "revolutionist," even the way he recollected the heroic aspects of his father's funeral, seem part of an effort to make his father conform to the tradition he was educated to, though he also understood that his father's revolutionary efforts were futile, doomed, and destructive, a lesson he had, in fact, learned at his father's knee.[36]

While Conrad's use of the Bobrowski posture in Part First served as a means of exculpation from the charge of desertion, it created a problem of a deeper sort that bloomed only momentarily for Conrad at page 204. There it opened the abyss for him between the most deeply split of his duplexities, that between Korzeniowski and Bobrowski. His youth had been a battle ground on which and, in a sense, over which this war was fought, and there was no arguable compromise between the two, no armistice, no peace, because, in reality, what was at stake was more a question of loyalties than of philosophies and could end only in confrontation and expiation, not in resolution. In Part First Haldin and Razumov clearly represent a distillation of those positions. There Haldin was a revolutionary catastrophe that happened to a Razumov of settled if untested views who defended himself by a betrayal that seemed forced on him. But if in this paradigm Haldin represented Apollo Korzeniowski and his views, Razumov represented not Tadeusz Bobrowski but a Conrad who had espoused Bobrowski's views. The superimposed *K* and *R* at page 204 is the first indication of this central dilemma that would eventually cause Conrad such despair as the writing progressed. For, given the paradigm he had created, he became his father's betrayer. The momentary confrontation at MS 204 with what his father represented would become a resident subject in the later portions of the novel, those that contain the *K*'s, where, by means of Razumov's contempt and disdain, Conrad mockingly betrays his father intellectually.

For example, during the conversation with Sophia, the *K*'s occur alongside two kinds of passages, ones in which the effects of Haldin's intrusion into Razumov's life are seen by his being put in false positions — forced to lie, placed on unsure ground, which opens him to insult — or ones in which he reacts contemptuously to the revolutionary type. They seem, in other words, to be Conrad's responses, either of blame for the effect his father's actions had upon him (loss of his corner of the world, being made contingent and, thus, inevitably put in false positions) or of disdain for the delusory quality of his father's ideas as an index of character.

Razumov is angered by being forced to lie: when Necator and Yaklovitch burst upon the scene on the grounds of the Chateau Borel, Necator making veiled accusations against Razumov, the latter is forced to lie and explodes,

"striking his fist into the palm of his other hand." Sophia
tries to quiet him. There is an elaborate *K* at the top of
the page 1049). She warns him that he must not carry on
like this else he shall go mad as he is angry with everybody
and bitter with himself and on the lookout for something to
torment himself with. He is so angry that he can only speak
in gasps: "It's intolerable! . . . . You must admit that I can
have no illusions on the attitude which . . . it isn't clear
. . . or rather . . . only too clear." He makes a gesture of
despair. "It was not his courage that failed him. [a large *K*
in the margin] The choking fumes of falsehood had taken
him by the throat — the thought of being condemned to
struggle on and on in that tainted atmosphere without the
hope of ever . . . . "(1053).

But it is while watching Sophia's self-deceptions, her
need to bend facts to fit preconceptions, that Razumov
is the most lucidly disdainful. For example, divining what
had happened to Ziemianitch would solve Sophia's quest to
know who had denounced Haldin, to know whether Razumov was one of them or a spy; but her belief in the mystical
goodness and power of the peasantry, parallel to Haldin's
and to Apollo Korzeniowski's, grossly misleads her, as it
had Haldin and Apollo. Each time Sophia asks Razumov
about a town peasant and the people of the house he lived
in, Conrad makes a *K* in the margin (1059, 1060, 1061). Fear-
ing a trap, Razumov tells a half truth: "The bold Ziemianitch. How could it have slipped my memory like this!
One of the last conversations we have had together." [large
K] " 'Then!' Sophia Semenovna clapped her hands. 'That
means that he [Haldin] was thinking of him very shortly before . . . . ' " Razumov asks her why Ziemianitch committed
suicide. "Remorse," she says. "Razumov opened his eyes
very wide at that, Sophia Antonovna's informant by listening to the [*K*] talk of the house . . . had managed to

come very near the truth"(1070); Razumov "felt the need of
perfect safety, with its [crossed out *K*] freedom from direct
lying." Still responding to Razumov's question, " 'The crea-
ture has done justice to himself,' the woman observed as if
thinking aloud. [*K*] " 'What? Ah, yes! Remorse,' Razumov
muttered with equivocal contempt"(1082).

Near the end of this section of the novel, Razumov
observes that Sophia and her informant, in trying to puz-
zle out what actually happened to Haldin and Ziemianitch,
kept "so close to the truth, departing from it so far in the
verisimilitude of thoughts and conclusions as to give one the
notion of the invincible nature of human error, a glimpse
into the utmost depths of self-deception." A marginal *K*
precedes the phrase. He had Razumov reflect "that a revolutionist [*K*] is seldom true to the settled type. All revolt is
the expression of strong individualism" (1035), which seems
to be a comment on his father who, if nothing else, was a
strong individualist not "true to the settled type."

This direct and cutting criticism of his father's ideas
and the way they illustrate his capacity to delude himself
is, in effect, an ongoing betrayal and is not made without a
tremor of guilt. Sophia asks him about his feelings on the
day of Haldin's arrest. "It was horrible; it was an atrocious
day. It was not the last," he answers. She replies that she
understands, that she knows how it feels: "One's ashamed
of being left." She adds, "And what is death? At any rate,
it is not a shameful thing like some kinds of life." Razumov,
stung by her phrase, feels a "feeble and unpleasant tremor"
stir in his breast. Opposite this passage is a *K*.

Tradition and common sense suggest that a major
source of guilt in males is the unresolved tensions between
fathers and sons, particularly if the father has departed before they could be worked out. Did Conrad have unresolved
feelings vis à vis his father? It would have been extraordi-

nary had he not, as they lived bound together in the isolation of exile during his most formative years. It is likely given the trauma of his mother's death, particulary as one of the commonest responses of children to the loss of a parent is a combination of anger and self-blame,[37] feelings which were surely complicated by Apollo's self-accusations, his growing Mariolatry of his wife, and the cult of death that suffused it. That Mariolatry was, in effect, an egocentric preoccupation which at times excluded Conrad from the life and death of the family and condemned him to a kind of neglect.[38] Even as a child he must have had very confused feelings about his father, for not only did he hear his father's *mea culpas*, he heard them reenforced by his uncle during sojourns with him to improve his poor health and nervousness, which were surely occasioned, at least in part, by his family's demise and his father's reactions. Bobrowski's criticisms of the father and praise for the angelic mother only served to validate Apollo's own words, and yet he he missed his father terribly during those periods away. Despite all this, Conrad and his father were very close, which could only make his anxieties more painful. Zdzisław Najder's observations are apt:

> Thus his father's heritage was for Conrad a cause of strong internal conflict. On the one hand he could not escape the powerful appeal of Apollo's fascinating personality and of the heroic fidelity with which he had served to the tragic end the ideals of patriotism as he had conceived them. On the other hand he was by no means sure if these ideals had had any reasonable basis. Conrad's father must have seemed to him at once awe-inspiring and absurd; his attitude towards him was a mixture of admiration and contemptuous pity. And he could never forgive his father the death of his mother (*CPB*, 11).[39]

Nor, it would seem, could he settle in his mind either the meaning of his father's life or the sense of his death. He remembered his father and his father's death more vividly than he did his mother's, but he was, of course, older then; and they had been thrown together in a way he had not known with his mother. He was attached to his father, missed him when he was away as a child visiting his uncle. He remembered the great white doors to his father's last room, going in to kiss his hand each evening, and waiting in dread for the inevitable.[40] But despite his affection, the ambiguities of tone in Conrad's account of his father's funeral suggest a profound puzzlement, an incapacity to accept fully that his father might have earned a heroic reputation: "This great silent demonstration seemed to me the most natural tribute in the world — not to the man but to the Idea."[41]

Despite all that has been written about Poland and Eliza Orzeskowa, it is 214zConrad's filial plight, losing his father when he was eleven and then having to choose between father and uncle, in effect being educated, required by circumstance, to repudiate his father with whom he knows he has much in common, that is the likeliest source of his ever-present and depressive guilt feelings. It is impossible to avoid Conrad's self-description: "Homo duplex has in my case more than one meaning,"(*CL*, III:89) by which he meant not only Polish and English, because even the genetic Polish identity, that little Konrad from whom sprang the man, the signifier for whom was *K*, was split between the Korzeniowski and Bobrowski families, between father and uncle, between the romance of messianic nationalism and the prudent acceptance of accountancy, between *szlachic* assumptions about ego and conduct and the facts of an insecure and traumatized childhood, between wanting to be an insider occupying his own corner of the world and being an outsider, an observer, always on unsure ground. Like Razumov, he struggled "in the toils of a false position." It is

not astonishing that Conrad's marginal *K*'s stop abruptly
with Razumov's written confession to Natalia, for it is at
that point that his "false position," the equivalent of Conrad's situation as *homo duplex*, is resolved. Razumov confesses that in giving up Haldin, it was himself that he had
betrayed, that the revolutionists have right on their side. It
is the equivalent of Conrad's recovering his father, accept-
ing him as a tragic figure rather than as rash, deluded, and
destructive (see pp. 18–19 of Keith Carabine's essay).

To recognize and accept the father in himself was to repudiate his uncle, his benefactor and surrogate father, and
to repudiate some part of what he wanted to believe about
himself. By cheating his uncle, that is, in this polarized
view, by acting like his father, he had done so. By being financially irresponsible in the present as he was writing this
novel, he continued to do so. But to accept his uncle's es-
timate was to repudiate his father and himself. His choices
were time bombs. It is from this nexus that derive the feeling of incurable guilt, the incompletions, the sense of being
blocked or directed by outside causes, of always being reac-
tive, and they emotionally drove this novel. The seeds were
there the moment he undertook to explain himself, for he
would inevitably accuse himself as he excused himself. In
this strange and depressive symbiosis, writing had become
as painful as analysis.

But painful as it might have been, this alternance between revealing and concealing, so deeply and firmly based
in his childhood, is the essence of Conrad's voice, of his
manner. One is reminded of Buffon's truth, "Le style c'est
l'homme même."

NOTES

I wish to express my thanks to a number of individuals and institutions: for grants which permitted me to study this and other Conrad manuscripts, the American Philosophical Society and the Andrew W. Mellon Foundation, the Division of the Humanities and Social Sciences of the California Institute of Technology and, over time, its chairmen, Hallett Smith, Robert Huttenback, Roger Noll, and David Grether; for access to the manuscript, the Beinecke Rare Book and Manuscript Library at Yale University and most particularly the wonderfully helpful Marjorie Grey Wynne; for access to the letters of the forthcoming fourth volume of the *Collected Letters*, Laurence Davies and Frederick R. Karl; for invaluable assistance in plotting the manuscript against the printed book, Harold McGee. I also wish to acknowledge a debt to my fellow contributors, most particularly Keith Carabine, for his generosity and engagement.

[1] Conrad opened this discussion regarding the confessional aspect of writing by accusing Rousseau, who was much on his mind because of the important role he would play in *Under Western Eyes*, of discrediting the confessional form by the thoroughness (read, the openness) with which he confessed and by his evident effort to justify himself. It is an interesting tirade on two counts. For one, the early portions of his novel are in some measure an effort at self-justification, an effort he does not wish to reveal and, perhaps, does not wish to recognize. For another, while admitting that the writer, by which he means "novelist," "stands confessed" in his works, he insists that little is revealed. According to this argument, Rousseau openly reveals his most personal secrets because he "had no imagination .... He was no novelist." Confessed though he may be, the novelist reveals little because he imaginatively creates what amounts to a parallel world. But the recurrence of this theme of non-revelation also suggests that it is closely tied to Conrad's *pudeur*, to his fear of public display.

[2] Letter to Harriet Capes, 13 May, 1909. Quoted in Najder, p. 342.

³ See note *4* to Keith Carabine's essay in this volume. This letter of 13 September 1911, Berg, "confirms that 'A Familiar Preface' . . . is of special relevance to *Under Western Eyes*."

⁴ On the versos of nearby sheets, Conrad also sketched a variety of hulls and riggings, an English handsome cab, and various denominations of British coins for the apparent purpose of explaining his life at sea and in Britain to his Polish family.

⁵ *JCC*, p. 161. *TTC*, p. 20. Richard Curle, *The Last Twelve Years of Joseph Conrad* (London: Sampson Low, Marston & Co., 1928), p. xx.

⁶ See *JCC*, p. 161. Najder also includes a photograph of the certificate of discharge in the illustrations.

⁷ Letter of Saturday [18? August 1894]. In *CL*, I, 108–110.

⁸ Citations from the manuscript will appear parenthetically without attribution. The corresponding sections of the printed novel are as follows: Part First, pp. 1–99 (ms 1–338); Part Second, pp. 100–197 (ms 339–806); Part Third, pp. 198–292 (ms 807–1123); Part Four, pp. 293–382 (ms 1123–1351).

⁹ "Officially and in fact without a family . . . , no home influences had shaped his opinions or his feelings. He was as lonely as a man swimming in the deep sea. The word Razumov was the mere label of a solitary individuality" (*UWE*, p. 10).

¹⁰ It was written in four stages: the first (ms 1–339/1–99) from December 1907 to mid-March 1908, the second (339–668/100–160) from mid-March to 13 October 1908, the third (666-898/160-226) from 14 October 1908 to 28 July 1909, and the fourth (898-1351/227-382) from 28 July 1909 to 22 January 1910. Keith Carabine has carefully worked out the stages of the composition by using Conrad's letters, dates jotted in the margins of the manuscript and the typescript. He has generously allowed me to use this chronology, which is still in manuscript form, but for a fuller description of these stages, see both his and David Leon Higdon's essays in this volume.

¹¹ *The Daily News*, 10 August 1908, quoted in Najder, p. 341, reprinted in Norman Sherry, *Conrad: The Critical Heritage* (London: 1973), pp. 210–211. Had Robert Lynd been Conrad's analyst, he could not have known better what the sore

points of his psyche were. The review was devastatingly smug, insular, nationalistic, and wrong-headed and surely aimed to hurt. "Mr. Conrad," he wrote, "without either country or language, may be thought to have found a new patriotism for himself in the sea. His vision of men, however, is the vision of a cosmopolitan, of a homeless person. Had he but written in Polish his stories would assuredly have been translated into English and into the other languages of Europe; and the works of Joseph Conrad translated from the Polish would, I am certain, have been a more precious possession on English shelves than the works of Joseph Conrad in the the original English." According to my colleague Elazar Barkan, xenophobia was running quite high in Britain in this period. Exclusionary immigration laws, based on those in effect in the U. S., had been passed in 1908 with the aim of keeping Asians and Eastern Europeans out. It was an atmosphere that could only have exacerbated Conrad's feelings of estrangement.

¹² Borys Conrad, *My Father: Joseph Conrad* (New York: Coward-McCann, 1970), p. 60.

¹³ 30 July 1909, Birmingham. Quoted in *JCC*, p. 352.

¹⁴ Conrad to Mackintosh, Easter Sunday, [11 April] 1909, Colgate. Quoted in *JCC*, p. 348. Conrad liked the phrase. In a letter to Pinker of Wednesday, [4? August 1909], Berg, quoted in *JCC*, p. 351, he wrote, "He's a megalomaniac who imagines that he is managing the Universe and that everybody treats him with the blackest ingratitude. A fierce and exasperating vanity is hidden under his calm manner which misleads people .... I do not hesitate to say that there are cases, not quite as bad, under medical treatment." Conrad's relationship with Ford was always volatile and strained. See his letter to Garnett of 31 March 1899: "I expected you and fate has sent Hueffer. Let this be written on my tombstone"(*CL*, II:177).

¹⁵ Berg collection. Quoted in *JCC*, p. 349.

¹⁶ Letter of 31 July 1909, in *LL*, II:101–102.

¹⁷ In a letter to Galsworthy, n.d., Birmingham. On 7 September 1909, also in Birmingham, he wrote Galsworthy, "A

Russian has got hold of the *ER* and I can not contribute any more." Quoted in *JCC*, p. 568.

[18] Keith Carabine and Owen Knowles checked with the Bank of England which informed them that the pound sterling has depreciated approximately sixty times since 1909, which would turn Conrad's £2,250 obligation into a 1989 debt of £135,000 or $216,000 (at 1.6 dollars to the pound). I do not know how the Bank of England derived its numbers, but even calculated differently, the equivalent sum is impressive. In 1909 there were 4.867 dollars to the pound: £2,250 equalled $10,950. Since 1909 the dollar has devalued 12.33 times, so $10,950 equal $135,014 or £84,383. This money was for living expenses for a period of somewhat more than two years, expenses which included heavy medical costs (Jesse's knees and Conrad's ongoing gout, influenza, depression, and so on) as well as Borys's schooling. The higher calculation suggests annual expenses of about $86,400, the lower of about $54,000, figures which are extravagant or not, according to one's bias. Whichever, he was very clearly not living in privation. [My thanks to Professor Lance Davis for the "American" calculations above, which are based on the following: The 4.867 ratio was a constant from the gold standard. The devaluation of the dollar was calculated from *Historical Statistics of the United States: Colonial Times to 1957*, Goverment Printing Office, Washington, D. C., 1960 and supplements. From 1960 to 1989, calculations were based on *Statistical Abstracts of the United States*, published annually by the Department of Commerce, Washington, D. C.]

[19] To Pinker, n.d. (end of July), Berg. In *JCC*, p. 340.

[20] To Percival Gibbon, 19 December [1909], repeated in another letter to him of Wednesday, [29 December 1909], Berg, in *JCC*, p. 355. He indulged in the same rhetoric in a letter to Galsworthy on 22 December 1909, Birmingham, quoted in Baines, pp. 359–360.

[21] Letter of 5 November 1912. In *LG*, p. 243. "The Secret Sharer" was written in late November and early December. Carabine dates these passages, that is ms 1314–1321, as from early January.

[22] The date, the 22nd of January, that he dashed across the bottom of sheet 1351 was like a breath of relief, an "ouf," he was so pleased to be done with it, which, of course, he was not, as he had to spend the next four days rewriting the ending. See Keith Carabine's essay in this volume.

[23] While he may have had certain of Hueffer's pretensions in mind at this point, it is more likely that his bias goes farther back. When he and his father were first out of exile, the latter looked carefully for a school for Conrad, one that had not been too Germanized, most particularly one which had not permitted the bastardizing of the Polish language. This defense of Slavic purity against the inroads of Germany and the West is another parallel with Dostoevsky.

[24] See Carabine's essay in this volume, particularly note *16*, in which he shows how Conrad attacked certain attitudes of his father's, notable Apollo's mystical belief in the peasantry.

[25] See *JCC*, pp. 35, 37, and Baines, pp. 28–30, for accounts of Conrad's difficulties with the orphanage director regarding his daughter.

[26] See Baines, pp. 68–69 for an account of Conrad bilking his uncle. Conrad "apparently wrote a letter dated 10 August to Bobrowski telling him that he had sailed in a ship which had been wrecked and that he had thus lost all his kit; he therefore asked urgently for £10." It was a crude but, given Bobrowski's response, colorful attempt: "I received your desperate letter yesterday evening and reply to it today with the remittance you want, in accordance with the maxim; '*Bis dat qui cito dat*', or 'Twice gives he who quickly gives' . . . . Thank God that you survived, that you're alive and only had a few days of illness in hospital — a desirable refuge this time — and that you emerged safely from that fatal adventure! I should have preferred, actually, that you had saved your things too together with your bones — but what's happened has happened, and we must reconcile ourselves to the fact and patch up your poverty as well as we can. Thus I enclose the £ you ask for, and I shall not deduct it from your October allowance. You can have it as an 'extra'. *as a mariner in distress* . . . ." Bobrowski goes on to wonder why

the shipowners, in negotiating with the insurors could not have got something for their officers' belongings. His hardheadedness was on the mark, for Conrad had never been on board the vessel in question and even got the name of it wrong (it was the *Annie Frost* not the *Anna Frost*), but it was exactly the kind of appeal to Bobrowski's good heart that would work.

²⁷ Italics indicate deletions in the manuscript, brackets indicate material added in the manuscript.

²⁸ It is a phrase Conrad seems to associate with the idea of dreaded inevitability, of unavoidable bad luck. Recalling his father's death and funeral, he says, "there was nothing in my aching head but a few words, some such stupid sentences as, "It's done." He had just previously written of his father's impending death: "I looked forward to what was coming with an incredulous terror. I turned my eyes from it sometimes with success, and yet all the time I had an awful sensation of the inevitable." In "Poland Revisited," *Notes on Life and Letters* (London: J. M. Dent & Sons, 1946), p. 225–226.

²⁹ It was a question much on his mind. In Chapter 2 of *APR*, p. 35, he writes, "for why should I, the son of a land which such men as these have turned up with their ploughshares and bedewed with their blood, undertake the pursuit of fantastic meals of salt junk and hard tack upon the wide seas? On the kindest view it seems an unanswerable question. Alas! I have the conviction that there are men of unstained rectitude who are ready to murmur scornfully the word desertion. Thus the taste of innocent adventure may be made bitter to the palate."

³⁰ Tadeusz Bobrowski's character is far too complex to be gone into here, but there is, I think, a tendency among many to regard him personally, despite his evident sense of family, simply as a Polonius with the soul of an accountant, and politically as a self-serving appeaser. He did enjoy his logic, winning arguments, and he did keep his accounts in order, but he was not lacking a genuine civic sense as can been seen in his efforts to help the peasantry by promoting the cultivation of sugar beets. Nowhere are the contradictions of his character more evident than in his "Memoirs" II:70 (translated in *CUFE*, pp. 28–29) where, with

some complacency, he described himself as "a convinced doctrinaire, deeply confident of the inflexibile and unchanging rights and duties of the mind, of critical judgement and free will which make man a master of his own fate and history; I reject all side influences issuing from emotions and passions and from other people; through clear thinking I have arrived at a ready formula to meet every problem in life." He was even pleased with the *rébarbatif* aspect of his character. "Sometimes, intentionally exaggerating my assertions, I used to enrage my uncle, stun Mr Zagórski and make my sister cry." But within a page of this he speaks with approval of landholders who treat their peasants with justice and appears to deplore those who oppress them.

[31] The image of Haldin's phantom lying in the snow across the track of Razumov's footprints is a curiously self-reflexive symbol that Razumov interprets in his own novel, for he understands that he has actually stepped over a symbol, and he knows what that means. For Conrad it is an intertextual symbol, which may account for its self-reflexivity, for he insists on this visual image of stepping over the phantom body of Haldin as, literally, the transgression, the symbol of the crime. Indeed, it is an oddly exact visual translation of the word "crime" (*prestuplenie*) in Russian, -as in *Crime and Punishment*. The root sense (*pre* indicating "over," *stup* deriving from "foot," and *lenie* indicating an action) is "stepping over."

[32] Conrad rewrote this short passage three times in order to achieve the sharpness of effect. The manuscript reads:

> then made Razumov's leaden
> *heart flew into his throat*
> heart *fly into his throat*. [strike a ponderous blow] by
> springing up briskly

Material in italics was deleted, in brackets added.

[33] See Avrom Fleishman, *Conrad's Politics* (Baltimore: The Johns Hopkins Press, 1967), p. 7.

[34] See Fleishman, pp. 5–6, and W. F. Reddaway *et al. The Cambridge History of Poland* (originally published in 1941; London: Cambridge University Press, 1950–1951), II:369–370, from which Fleishman quotes extensively.

[35] Fleishman, p. 5. He describes Korzeniowski's career as "vigorous, headlong, and brief."

[36] See his "Author's Note" to the 1919 republication of *A Personal Record.*

[37] See particularly Martha Wolfenstein, "Loss, Rage, and Repetition," *Psychoanalytic Study of the Child*, v. 24, 1969, pp. 432–460, also by the same author, "How Is Mourning Possible," *Psychoanalytic Study of the Child*, v. 21, 1966, pp. 93–123.

[38] In Apollo's well-known letters to Kazimierz Kaszewski from 26 and 28 February 1865, he writes at length about Ewa's illness, the lack of treatment, their misery and despair. "We are very miserable and unhappy — but we praise God for letting us carry our destiny together .... And all this has resulted from unity — not of ideas but of principles; from unity -- not of tastes but of a sense of duty." But he hardly mentions his son, and then only to say, "Konradek is of course neglected." It is easy to overdetermine the meaning of this sort of information, but much that we learn of his boyhood suggests a kind of alienation. He hardly remembers his mother, he tells Kazimierz Waliszewski on 5 December, 1903, and yet he was seven and a half when she died. On the one hand, one may suppose that he repressed his memories of a traumatized childhood, but on the other, we may also suppose that he was pushed aside, particularly by Apollo's hectic and guilty need to deal with himself.

[39] *CPB*, p. 11. Najder's last two sentences ("Conrad's father must have seemed to him at once awe-inspiring and absurd; his attitude towards him was a mixture of admiration and contemptuous pity. And he could never forgive his father the death of his mother.") are curious, seem reasonable, though the second clause of the first of these sentences and the second sentence entire escape the suppositive quality of the first clause and pass as fact.

[40] *NLL*, "Poland Revisited," p. 225–226.

[41] "The Author's Note," written in 1919 for the republication of *APR*, p. viii. "As a child of course I knew very little of my father's activities, for I was not quite twelve when he died. What I saw with my own eyes was the public funeral, the cleared

streets, the hushed crowds; but I understood perfectly well that this was a manifestation of the national spirit seizing a worthy occasion. That bareheaded mass of work people, youths of the University, women at the windows, school-boys on the pavement, could have known nothing positive about him except the fame of his fidelity to the one guiding emotion in their hearts. I had nothing but this knowledge myself; and this great silent demonstration seemed to me the most natural tribute in the world — not to the man but to the idea."

"Complete But Uncorrected": The Typescript of Conrad's *Under Western Eyes*

David Leon Higdon

Probably no letter concerning *Under Western Eyes*, Conrad's ninth novel, is more tantalizingly ambiguous, more direct in analysis, and more domestically frustrated than Jessie Conrad's 6 February 1910 letter to David Meldrum, in which she reports,

> The novel is finished but the penalaty [sic] has to be paid. Months of nervous strain have ended in a complete nervous breakdown. . . . There is the M.S. complete but uncorrected and his fierce refusal to let even I touch it. It lays on a table at the foot of his bed and he lives mixed up in the scenes and holds converse with the characters (*LBM*, 192).

The letter challenges biographers with its causal linkage of the composition of the novel and the breakdown, psychological critics with its image of a novelist so possessed by his characters that he "holds converse" with them, oblivious of the world around him, and textual scholars with its use of the word "manuscript," which still in 1910 and later meant either holograph manuscript or typescript, leaving one uncertain whether Jessie Conrad refers to the 1351 page holograph, the long-missing typescript which only reappeared in 1980, or some combination of both.[1] Scholars have long surmised that many of the mysteries surrounding this novel and its creator between 4 December 1907 when the short story which would become the novel was first mentioned by Conrad and 5 October 1911 when the novel was published by Methuen could be unlocked if the typescript were available for study, especially those mysteries, seemingly repeating the experiences of *Lord Jim* and *The Secret Agent*, when a recalcitrant story idea aggressively expanded to uncertain lengths as the original conception refused to accept narrower confines.

During the 24–25 April 1928 sale of the Edward Garnett collection, the public briefly glimpsed this most important and most elusive item. The catalogue of the sale advertised it as an "EXTREMELY IMPORTANT TYPESCRIPT REPLETE WITH ALTERATIONS IN THE AUTHOR'S HAND" and described two layers of revision "in ink and in blue pencil," in which Conrad "scored out" paragraphs and pages, "heavily corrected" sheets, gave "marginal directions to the typist," and added a holograph manuscript scene to the concluding chapter.[2] A facsimile of a typescript page in the catalogue bore out these promises of bibliographical riches, having had twenty of its twenty-five lines cancelled and seven holograph lines added.[3] The typescript attracted considerable attention, ultimately selling to Gabriel Wells for $2200, a noticeable appreciation in value since a similar typescript of *Almayer's Folly*, Conrad's first novel, fetched only $650 in the 1923 John Quinn sale, though still far less than the $4000 the *Victory* typescript would draw in the 1929 Jerome Kern sale.[4] Following the sale, the typescript promptly disappeared from both public and scholarly view. Its rediscovery late in 1980 now provides answers to a number of questions concerning the growth of the text, the writing habits Conrad had evolved by mid-career, and the effect of Conrad's 1910 breakdown on the revision of the novel.

The thirty months during which *Under Western Eyes* was written and revised — December 1907 to May 1910 — were the most troubled and in some ways are the least understood period in Conrad's career. Eighteen years after writing the opening sentences of *Almayer's Folly* on a September morning in 1889, Conrad approached his fiftieth birthday racked by physical and psychological difficulties. Troubled by mounting debts to his agent, James B. Pinker, by crumbling friendship with Ford Madox Hueffer, and by seeming inability to bring major works to closure, Conrad entered that crucial moment in mid-life when a male both reviews and reappraises the accomplishments of his early adulthood, deals with the polarities creating divisions within his life, and begins to modify his existing life structure. The retrospective nature of Conrad's letters during these months is striking and follows the pattern discerned by Daniel J. Levinson who noted that "a man's review of the past goes on in the shadow of the future. His need to reconsider the past arises in part from a heightened awareness of his mortality and a desire to use the remaining time more wisely."[5] What Conrad saw disturbed him greatly. In terms typical of such agonizing reappraisals, he wrote John Galsworthy, 6 January 1908, stressing his financial failure, his inability to secure an audience (a telling point since 1908 would bring him only £5)[6], and his illnesses:

> Eleven novels. If each had averaged £1000 I would have now 500 in hand. For counting up all I owe you, other debts, the balance against me with P[inker] (1572 to date) and this grant I had together with all I have earned it works out at £650 p year in round numbers. Even if I have made a mistake of a 100 a year too little which is improbable (for however carelessly I counted I am not likely to have underestimated all I had by 1200 pounds st[erling]) this is

not outrageously extravagant. And in this there's Jessie's illness, all of my own — (the year wasted when writing Nostromo when I had six fits of gout in eleven months) — and this fatal year with Borys abroad.[7]

In some desperation, he wrote Pinker about setting aside *Chance* and making a serious attempt at popular success:

> As I've told you my mind runs very much on popularity just now. I would try to reach it not by sensationalism but by means of taking a widely discussed subject for the *text* of my novel (*CL*, III:439).[8]

And on 3 August, he even envisioned completing *Chance* by December 1907: "I cling to it desperately. It must be done! And another *novel must* be finished by August next. I have got the idea in my head. A good idea too" (*CL*, III:462). The shrill, almost hysterical tone of these letters is obvious and the impossibility of the deadlines clearly evident, since they would have had Conrad writing no less than 180,000 words in twelve months.

Indeed, Conrad seemed further than ever from securing financial success and the reading public he felt his talents should have earned him. His talents, moreover, suddenly came under attack. Reviews of *The Secret Agent* in late 1907 had not been enthusiastic. Israel Zangwill, for example, criticized both the novel and its author, calling Conrad "a writer with a personality as egotistical as that of Mr. Bernard Shaw, only lacking in the wit and humour which goes some way to justify the existence of the latter," and the following year *A Set of Six* elicited reviews from Robert Lynd and W. L. Courtney in the 21 September 1908 *Daily News* and the 10 August 1908 *Daily Telegraph* which criticized Conrad on two extremely sensitive points — his English prose style and his foreign background.[9] Straining for effect rather than meaning, pushing rhetoric far beyond sense, Lynd had commented:

Had [Conrad] but written in Polish his stories would assuredly have been translated into English and into the
other languages of Europe; and the works of Joseph Conrad translated from the Polish would, I am certain, have
been a more precious possession on English shelves than
the works of Joseph Conrad in the original English, desirable as these are. What greater contribution has been made
to literature in English during the past twenty years than
Mrs. Constance Garnett's translations of the novels of Turgenieff? But suppose Turgenieff had tried to write them in
English!

Rightly infuriated with this nonsense, Conrad wrote Galsworthy, his sentences arctically sarcastic:

The above Dly News genius exclaims that my novels would
have been much better if translated by Mrs. Garnett. That's
an idea. Shall I send her the clean type of Razumov? But
why complicate life to that extent? She ought to write
them; and then the harmless reviewer could begin something like this: "Mr Joseph Conrad's latest novel written
by Mrs Garnett is a real acquisition for our literature, not
like the others previously published which on the whole
were rather noxious if amazing phenomena. . . ."[10]

His works and worth impugned by such reviewers, his pro-
ductivity questioned by his agent/banker, and his creativity
tortured by his own inner doubts, Conrad finally collapsed
during the last week of January 1910, deliriously talking to
his characters in Polish, unable to work — paralyzed, he
had earlier written to James Gibbons Huneker, by "a sort
of horror of pen and ink, a mistrust of the written phrase
[which] sets on me like a cold nightmare."[11]

The turbulent years between 1907 and 1910, however,
saw the publication of *The Secret Agent* and *A Set of Six*,
the composition of *Under Western Eyes, Some Reminiscences,* "The Secret Sharer," "Prince Roman," a trenchant
essay on censorship, several reviews, and much of *Chance*,
but our understanding of the nature of the creation of *Un-*

der Western Eyes has been seriously handicapped by missing documents, mainly the typescript. As a result, several assumptions about the composition have become prevalent in discussions of the novel, and each of these assumptions must now be tested in light of the new evidence. For example, it has been assumed that Conrad worked more or less continuously from 1907 until 1910 on the text, that he may have deliberately withheld passages while writing, that Galsworthy's reaction to a long section of Part Second led to the cancellation of three long scenes, that Conrad had significant difficulties in achieving appropriate closure for the novel, that a major revision involving cuts of almost 30,000 words occurred between the serial and the first edition, and that the text was essentially unrevised before the breakdown.[12] Because the manuscript and the first edition of the novel differ so dramatically, surely the keys to further understanding of the years and their creative activities, greater awareness of the nature of the crisis, and the practical matter of knowing precisely how and when work on *Under Western Eyes* progressed are contained in this document.

The manuscript of *Under Western Eyes*, item 1862 in the John Quinn sale, has always been considered more newsworthy than the typescript, even though it poses more questions than it answers.[13] There is an undeniable mystique to the holograph manuscript of any author, perhaps because one intuits that he has come closer to touching actual creativity, an assumption of questionable validity when an artist regards his manuscript as a rough draft. The *Under Western Eyes* manuscript, moreover, has been readily available for study, and its interpretative implications well documented in three perceptive, if not definitive, statements. Eloise Knapp Hay has studied its cancelled passages relating to political topics and has also noted the obvious references to Leo Tolstoy and Feodor Dostoyevsky; Roderick Davis has concentrated on the cancellations replete with autobiographical significance; and Emily K. Izsak [Dalgarno] has focused on "Conrad's habits of thought and work" as well as on "an essential contradiction in the satirical characterization of Peter Ivanovitch" and "an interpretation of Razumov's 'diary' more modern in tone than that of the published version."[14] At the Quinn auction, the manuscript sold for an astonishing $6900 to Jerome Kern, second only to the $8100 fetched by the *Victory* manuscript. Six years later, in the Kern sale, the *Under Western Eyes* manuscript brought $7250, an investment appreciation of only $350, its buyer, Gabriel Wells, perhaps intrigued by the totally misleading catalogue description: "THE ORIGINAL MANUSCRIPT OF THIS STORY, which differs so materially from the printed version as the story progresses, in the arrangement of the chapters, dialogues, paragraphs, and phrases, because Conrad worked over it and deleted many portions before the copy was ready for the printer."[15] This manuscript eventually was donated to the Beinecke Rare Book and Manuscript Library at Yale University, where, one assumes, it will remain.

Once purchased by Gabriel Wells, though, the typescript enjoyed no such public history or availability. A Hungarian immigrant and master of eight languages, Wells was surely one of the more colorful and secretive of the New York collectors and dealers. He guarded his clients' privacy and perhaps his own profits, it was rumored, by keeping no written records. His purchases often passed quietly into private collections, but he also generously donated items to libraries, bequeathing to Rutgers University Library, for instance, first editions of *The Faerie Queene* and *The history of Don-Quichote*, a Shakespeare second folio, a 1479 Justinus, and other items.[16] At some point before his death in

1946, he sold the *Under Western Eyes* typescript to Richard
S. Gimbel of Philadelphia, whose estate donated it in December 1977 along with several other Conrad items including a typescript of *Victory* and a rich treasure of other valuable manuscripts, typescripts, and editions to the Philadelphia Free Library.[17]

A number of questions are posed immediately by the
typescript. What kind of document is it? How is it related
both to the manuscript and to the printed texts? What
does it tell us about *Under Western Eyes* that we do not already know from the manuscript, letters, and other sources?
What does it reveal about Conrad's work habits, especially
his revision habits? And, finally, what light can it shed on
those troubled years which, in the view of many scholars,
mark a significant dividing line in Conrad's career? The
typescript, it should quickly be noted, provides answers to
a number of lesser but quite revealing questions. There can
be no doubt, for example, that Conrad saw Razumov as a
tragic figure, but to what extent was Conrad actually aware
of theories of tragedy? Is his description of Mrs. Haldin
— "She was one of those natures, rare enough, luckily, in
which one cannot help being interested, because they provoke both terror and pity" (*UWE*, 318) — a fortuitous repetition of the key Aristotelian terms or a conscious allusion?
The typescript, and only the typescript, clearly reads: "as
Aristotle has said, both terror and pity" (TS, P2.6),[18] indicating that Conrad moved from an unspecified allusion
to a specified allusion and then restored the original reading, a feature of his revisions in the typescript. Then, too,
what reader has not puzzled over the subject of the essay
with which Razumov hopes to win the Silver Medal and,
more important, to secure his future? The manuscript and
all eight states of printed texts, remain maddeningly un-
specific; the typescript specifies: "and first of all get that

silver medal. It was the prize essay on the Civil Reform of Peter the Great that he had been writing during that period of seclusion, with a flying pen, as if from inspiration" (TS, N20.11-21.2). The statue of Jean-Jacques Rousseau, so important to the political and intellectual subtexts of the novel is a typescript addition (M14.10), as is the conspicuous foregrounding of Razumov's symbolic watch when it reappears in Part Four (N18.3-4). Solutions to Razumov's plight, however, are struck from the typescript, erasing his plans to hide by transferring to a provincial university (N19.13-20.4 and N23.9). The majority of revisions refine phrasing, reshape thematic references, delete specific backgrounds or emotions, correct mistypings or misphrasings, or add punctuation — changes made at the level of the individual sentence and largely unrelated by any discernible, overarching plan or conception. In addition to changing Sophia Semenovna to Sophia Antonovna (P24.5) a number of times to "disinfect" the noticeable influence of Dostoyevsky on the text, Conrad simply polished numerous sentences, for example, by revising a description of Laspara on a stool from "feet entwined" to "feet twisted" (M5.10) to emphasize the grotesque features of the revolutionaries, changed "remain like that for a few hours" to "remain for hours holding" (N13.3) to capture Tekla's abilities more emotively, allowed Razumov's thoughts to expand from the mere "young" to "young. Everything can be lived down" (N23.9), a thought whose falsity increasingly haunts Razumov, and, in an unfortunate unfolding of an image, turned "the stony stillness of her mother" to "the terrible immobility of her mother, who seemed to watch a beloved head lying in her lap" (T2.11). The revisions occurring on larger scales involve deletions of passages involving the narrator's relationship with the various characters in the first two parts of the novel and extensive reshaping of the materials in packets J, N, O, and T, which treat the confrontations in Part Four between Razumov and Mikulin and Razumov's confession to Natalia and her mother.

The typescript itself consists of twenty-six bradded "packets," ranging from ten to eighty-seven pages in length and totalling 841 leaves (843 pages; see Tables One and Two). The first five and the last of these packets are un-labeled, though they have consecutive pagination; the re-maining twenty have been labelled A through T, a practice Conrad also used with *Chance* and *Victory*.[19] The packets account for all but two paragraphs of the printed text, and, in addition, contains much heavily revised and cancelled material.[20] There appears to be no logic to the bradding of the packets: packets rarely coincide with the ends of scenes or divisions of parts, often beginning or breaking off in mid-sentence, a practice similar to the packets of manuscript which Conrad sent to the typist, though there is no corre-lation between the packets and the directions to the typist in the manuscript. Only 125 (14.82%) of the pages show no authorial revision; 690 (81.85%) have been revised, some-times quite extensively, and 28 (3.32%) are newly added holograph pages. Five different kinds of paper — Oceana Superfine, Excelsior Superfine, Rock Leigh Mill, Fine Com-mercial, and many sheets not watermarked — comprise the typescript. Types of paper, spacing of lines, distribution of revisions, and colors of ink and pencil indicate that the typescript is very much a composite document, extensively revised and highly polished in some sections but only a step away from holograph draft in others. Much of the typescript is clear and readable, but a number of the carbon pages have faded and browned to the extent that they can be read only with difficulty. Dating from October 1908, Pack-ets [1-5], the first 312 pages, are double-spaced, quite close to the printed text, and free of extensive revisions other than cancelled passages, paragraphs, and pages. Packets A-C begin immediately after the "clean copy," continue its double-spacing until C14, and lead up to the scene in which Razumov appears in Geneva, the scene which posed the first major impasse for Conrad. These three packets are double-spaced, except for the last thirteen pages of Packet C. The remaining typed pages in packets D-T are triple spaced with wide margins, show more extensive revisions within individual sentences, and often differ tellingly from the printed text. Packets J–T are variously dated from 24 September 1909 to 29 January 1910. Obviously, the early packets are clean copy, virtually ready for the printer, while the later packets, prepared on cheap, unwatermarked paper, are working typescript. This assumption is borne out by Conrad's direction to his typist: "All the pages are in sequence and the batches are lettered. Please carry on the numbering of the clean copy. This is the end of part II containing end of Chap IV and Chapter V" (TS, A1. This A1 comes at the end of Packet T and is not to be confused with the A1 in Packet A.). Also, a 1910 letter to Robert S. Garnett confirms that the Philadelphia typescript was used to generate clean copy. On 7 April, Conrad wrote: "I send you this batch trusting to your kindness to have it put in hand at some good typing office. Another lot will follow in a few days but I cant [*sic*] yet work even at this sort of thing for longer than one hour at a time."[21] A week later, Conrad requested that if Garnett felt "inclined to look at the stuff at all you will use the shortened copy such as I mean it to appear serially."[22] Throughout the typescript, Conrad revised in black ink, blue pencil, and black lead pencil, and it is easily demonstrable that these represent three different layers of revision done at different times. Passage after passage has been revised in black ink or, less frequently, in lead pencil, only to be cancelled later in blue indelible pen-

cil during the "reckless cutting" of 1910. The forty-seven
pages entirely cancelled in Part Second, for instance, were
extensively revised in black ink before being struck by blue
pencil slashes. These layers are undoubtedly the "three superimposed revisions" Conrad mentioned in a 17 May 1910
letter to Galsworthy.[23]

We have long known from extant letters that a typescript version of *Under Western Eyes* began to come into
existence almost simultaneously with the manuscript, creation and revision stages overlapping significantly.[24] In December 1907, Conrad told Pinker that he had "10 pp. of
Razumov, the first of the two short stories" in hand, and
by 30 December he had given Pinker at least forty more
pages for typing.[25] By 2 January, Conrad had completed
the text to page 70. Eight or ten more pages followed on 7
January 1908; more in February, 9 pages "to the end of Ch.
IV" on 12 March,[26] or up to manuscript page 418. By May,
though, Conrad admitted to Pinker that the story was out
of hand; he wrote: "I can't let you have Razumov yet. That
story must be worked out as it is worth it."[27] By July 1908,
Conrad was exploring the possibility of having a typist at
his home who "could take down a story and *at the same
time* begin typing a clean copy of *Razumov*. The present
type is so interlined that I don't like to show it even to you
[Pinker]. . . . But I must first have my story arranged in
my head and get nearer the end with Razumov."[28] On 29
September 1908, Miss Lillian Hallowes joined the Conrad
household at Someries in Bedfordshire. She was to prepare
clean copy of approximately 62,000 words of "Razumov,"
a task which she completed by 8 October.[29] Chapters I, II,
and III were sent to Pinker 13 October, and Chapters IV, V,
and VI were promised as following in "to-morrow evening's
post."[30] Chapters IV, V, VI, and part of VII were mailed
14 October to join the "good sample."[31] Through the end

of Chapter VI would have taken Hallowes to page 618 of the manuscript and to page 287 of the typescript, in other words to that scene in Part Second when the narrator goes walking with Natalia in the gardens and meets Razumov, who returns to the narrative for the first time in Part Second. This particular scene seems to have been the major stumbling block for Conrad in terms of the reshaping of his original plans.

Conrad's habits of composition in mid-career, habits which mark his typescripts as often being more valuable to the history of the texts than the manuscripts, have not always been fully understood nor appreciated. Fourteen years earlier in 1894, Conrad completed most of *Almayer's Folly* before having a typescript prepared although evidence suggests he had used an intermediate typescript for the first six chapters.[32] In 1908, though, his habits follow a more regulated pattern. First come scenes, characters, narration, and a holograph draft; the manuscript is then turned into an intermediate typescript, usually in two copies, with widely spaced lines and generous margins allowing for, indeed, even inviting, revisions; finally, this revised typescript generates clean copy, ready for Pinker, publishers, and printers. Forty-three marginal notes appear in the manuscript, ranging from "One copy" to the more usually polite "2 copies today, please" or "1 copy tomorrow please" to an urgent "I copy as soon as possible."[33] Conrad requested two typed copies for the first 254 manuscript pages, comprising most of Part First and extending well into its section III, but only one copy of the next 500 or so pages. The last direction to the typist appears on MS729, six hundred pages from the end. Conrad outlined his practice in a 24 or 25 November 1908 letter to Pinker thus: "Tomorrow I shall send you 2 to 3 thou words more of *interlined* type to be *clean copied* (with carbon set) for the set. I find that I can (for the

present at any rate) save sending you the *pen MS* for intermediate typing. My wife finds time to do that. Therefore
whenever you get interlined type you may take it that it is
ready for final copy (and carbon). But should you get *pen
MS* then please have one typed copy only made and sent
back for my corrections."[34]

By good fortune, five pages of this interlined, intermediate typescript still exist, interleaved as replacements
for manuscript pages 440-41, 447-48, 842, 899, and 1267A.
The last two of these pages are virtually identical with
their corresponding pages in the Philadelphia typescript;[35]
the others differ so emphatically as to suggest that perhaps two typescript states, at least in the early portions of
the novel, intervene between manuscript and Philadelphia
typescript. For example, the TS leaves, double-numbered
175 and 178 (typed) and 440–41, 447–48 (handwritten),
come from the narrator's encounter with Peter Ivanovitch
at Natalia Haldin's Boulevard des Philosophes apartment.
The first involves Peter's meeting with the Siberian woman,
who, with the help of her blacksmith husband — the "obviously symbolic couple" (*UWE*, 124) sardonically mentioned
by the narrator — frees him from his chains; the second
concerns the narrator's assessment of Peter's relationship
with the Haldins (*UWE*, 126). Leaf 178/447-48 begins in mid-
sentence and contains ten cancelled lines and seven lines of
holograph addition. The leaf reads:[36]

> before, he had given up the ladies Haldin —
> no doubt reluctantly *for there could be no question of
> his being a determined person. It was perhaps to*
> be expected that he should *re-appear again* on this
> *terrible* occasion; after all he was their
> compatriot, *a refugee of mark and capable of
> understanding clearly. He would be able a
> Russian and a revolutionist to say the right
> thing, to strike the true, perhaps a*

*comforting note. But I did not like to see
him sitting there.* I trust an old man's
jealousy of mental influence has nothing to
do with it. I *made no claim* to influence,
still less to a special standing for my
silent friend*ship. R*emoved by the differences
of age and nationality *as if into the sphere* of
another existence; *it* produced even upon myself
the effect of being *a dumb helpless ghost,
an immaterial being that could only hover about*
in anxious concern *near a tenderly regarded* life
it can neither protect nor guide by as much as
a [whisper. As Miss Haldin, with her sure instinct
had refrained from introducing me to the burly
celebrity I would have retired quietly and
returned later on, had I not met a peculiar
expression in her eyes which I interpreted as
a request.]

The corresponding page in the Philadelphia typescript
reads:

before, he had given up the ladies Haldin — no doubt re-
luctantly for there could be no question of his being a determined person. It was perhaps to be expected that he
should re-appear again on this terrible occasion, as a Russian and a revolutionist, to say the right thing, to strike
the true, perhaps a comforting note. But I did not like to
see him sitting there. I trust that an unbecoming jealousy
of my privileged position had nothing to do with it. I made
no claim to a special standing for my silent friendship. Removed by the difference of age and nationality, as if into the
sphere of another existence, *I* produced even upon myself
the effect of a dumb helpless ghost, of an anxious immaterial thing that could only hover about without the power
to protect or guide by as much as a whisper. Since Miss
Haldin, with her sure instinct had refrained from introducing me to the burly celebrity, I would have retired quietly
and returned later on, had I not met a peculiar expression
in her eyes which I inter- preted as a request . . . (TS 178)

The differences are numerous but not highly significant, except for the striking number of restorations: tone, meaning, and even arrangement remain essentially the same, but the disappearance of most of two sentences and the crucial recasting of another indicate that further revision and perhaps yet another typescript — at least of this page — separate the two extant documents, one perhaps dictated by Conrad to Miss Hallowes. He did dictate *Some Reminiscences* and considered doing so for parts of "Razumov." Borys Conrad recalled a scene in their home very similar to that of Peter Ivanovitch dictating to Tekla: Lillian Hallowes, he remembered,

> was a good typist and possessed the ability to sit silent and motionless in front of her machine, hands resting tranquilly in her lap, for long periods, reacting promptly to a word, a phrase, or a sudden outburst of continuous speech, hurled at her abruptly as he prowled about the room or sat hunched up in his big armchair, as he dictated directly onto the typewriter.[37]

Typing, retyping, and retyping yet again seem more likely to explain the differences between the pages, and an August 1908 letter, two months before Hallowes joined the household, confirms that this was Conrad's practice during the first year of *Under Western Eyes.* He wrote Pinker:

> Will you please settle this little bill for repairs of typewriter. My wife wants to type the two clean copies of Razumov herself if you will send me a packet of typing paper and a couple of sheets of carbon paper. She will begin at once so that by the time the novel is done the copies will be ready at less cost than typing generally amounts to. Meantime I will be sending you the MS for the first type, unless she finds that she can manage that too.[38]

With the relationship between typescript and manuscript clearer, it becomes necessary to establish just when the existing typescript was prepared. On 4 December 1907, Conrad told Pinker that he was "trying to start a short story. It's the one about the revolutionist who is blown up with his own bomb," (*CL*, III:513) probably the first identifiable reference to "Razumov." By Monday, 12 or 19 December, Conrad mailed the first ten pages of the story to Pinker and indicated that he planned to send "the *rest* (say 35 pp)" the following Monday or Tuesday, which he apparently did on 23 December, with another twenty on 30 December (*CL*, III:515). The manuscript, thus begun in early December 1907, would not be completed until twenty-six months later on 22 January 1910, the date inscribed almost triumphantly across the bottom of the final page of the manuscript. One cannot assume from this, however, that the manuscript progressed steadily or continuously, for it appears that most of *Under Western Eyes* was actually written in fifteen months in two separate bursts of creativity, the first coming between December 1907 and September 1908, the second lasting from August 1909 until January 1910.

Between her arrival the last week in September 1908 and 14 October, Miss Hallowes proved herself a most efficient typist, having completed clean copy of Chapters I through VI (MS618/TS287) and "some" of Chapter VII, while Conrad superintended and corrected. She apparently remained in the household until some time in November, left, and then returned 4 December. Quite likely, she completed the typescript through page 312 (marked 313; MS668). As the various pieces of evidence fall together, we can see that between the first week of October 1908 and mid-May 1909, Conrad wrote 272 pages of manuscript and was obviously having considerable difficulties in restoring Razumov to the narrative and to his priorities as the novel's protagonist. Indeed, as late as 25 November 1908, Conrad apparently still thought that he could bring the work to closure relatively soon, for he wrote Pinker that he would "concentrate [him]self on Raz'v's last pages. I must do a lot of thinking."[39] The two interview scenes between the narrator and Razumov which close Part Second and between Peter Ivanovitch which comes early in Part Third taxed Conrad's ingenuity, and I hazard the speculation that Razumov's "day of many conversations" (*UWE*, 237) was an inspired instance of extemporized narration drawn out until Conrad had vented his dislike of revolutionaries and saw that he could write Part Fourth by repeating much of Part First with the central roles inverted.[40] In early January 1909, Conrad asked Pinker for "*one* typed copy of these pages (up to No700 in MS)."[41] These pages in Packet A indicate that Conrad had writen only thirty-two pages since Miss Hallowes prepared clean copy. He asked Pinker for the return of typed copy for manuscript pages 763-91 on 7 March 1909, and mentioned manuscript page 890 to James G. Huneker in an 18 May 1909.[42] After fallow time in May and June because of illness, Conrad wrote Norman Douglas, "Not a word written!"[43] It is fairly easy to trace the progress of the manuscript and typescript during 1909, because Professor Keith Carabine has demonstrated and Professor Laurence Davies has confirmed that the five dates in the manuscript — 4AP (MS792), 31 MCH (MS818), 8 MY (MS842), 24JU (MS879), and 28 JULY (MS899) — are dates written in Pinker's office when batches of manuscript arrived for typing.[44]

In other words, Part First and much of Part Second were completed, with clean copy prepared and black-ink revisions made by the end of 1908, and the rest of Part Second was written between November 1908 and March 1909. Moreover, the vexing matter of what John Galsworthy actually read may be solved. Sometime after 25 November 1908, clean copy was given to Galsworthy for scrutiny; Conrad was most insistent in his request that Pinker "kindly send [Galsworthy] the corrected copy (*not* carbon) of my novel." [45]

On 30 November 1908, Conrad responded to Galsworthy's critique:

> I am ever so glad that you find *Raz* interesting. Your criticism as to the IId part is the very echo of my own worrying thought. And yet . . .
> You see, it is all part of the general crookedness of my existence. You will not be surprised to hear that the doing of the Ist part has been very difficult. What you see is the residue of very many pages now destroyed, but by no means wasted from an unmaterial point of view. But good work takes time: to invent an action, a march for the story which could have been dispensed with part IId as it stands, was a matter of meditation, of trying and retrying for goodness knows how long. This I could not afford to do. I went on the obvious lines and on these lines I developed my narrative to give it some sort of verisimilitude. In other words I offered to sell my soul for half a crown — and now I have neither the soul nor the coin — for the novel is not finished yet. A fool's bargain — no great matter when one is young but at my age such passages embitter and discourage one beyond expression. I have no heart to think of compressing anything, for I have no illusion as to the quality of the stuff. The thing is "bad-in- itself". It should not be there at all. [46]

Work on the novel was interrupted in late 1908 and early 1909 by a number of things. First, Conrad took on a totally new project, escaping from "Razumov" in much the same way he had used "Razumov" as an escape from work on *Chance*: "I had to get away from *Chance*, with which I was making no serious progress," he told Galsworthy in a 6 January 1908 letter (*LL*, II:65). Similarly, he turned to "The Secret Sharer" in December 1909 for further escape from "Razumov." [47] The new project involved dictation of *Some Reminiscences* and immersion in the planning of the first issues of the *English Review*. Jessie Conrad recalled

the chaos of October and November 1908, and Conrad later
queried of Ford, "Do you care to be reminded that the editing of the first number was finished in that farmhouse we
occupied near Luton?"[48] A move from Someries to Aldington followed early in January 1909, further disrupting the
household and productive writing. Ironically, Razumov's
own writing experiences just such an interruption, sparked
into life again only by the chance words of Julius Laspara.

Late summer and fall 1909 seem to have brought a
frenzied new round of creativity. On 9 August 1909, Conrad informed Pinker that Perceval Gibbon had given him
"access to his Russian notes which is just what I wanted to
give me the tone of the last part."[49] The traumatic break
with Ford, dissociation from the *English Review*, and attacks of gout and neuralgic afflictions were momentarily
past, and a totally new series of dates appear in Part Third
and Part Four of the typescript. Packet J, which begins approximately halfway through Part Third, carries two dates,
24 September and 2 October; K, 16 October; L, 29 October;
M, 12 and 19 November; N, undated; O, 27 November: P,
4 December; Q, 21 or 31 December; and packets R, S, and
T are clearly dated 15, 27, and 29 January 1910.[50] These
ten packets comprise 324 pages (38.43% of the typescript),
and when the twenty-five pages of holograph are added,
this figure rises to 349 (41.40%). It appears that Conrad
maintained the rhythm he started as long ago as *Almayer's
Folly* when its first eight chapters were written between
1889 and 1891, while its last three chapters were written
between 6 December 1893 and 24 April 1894. The last two
parts of the novel appear, thus, to have raced typescript
against manuscript, with the typescript being completed
only a week after the manuscript, ironically according to
the plan Conrad announced to Pinker in the August 1908
letter quoted earlier.

The most frequently cited statement concerning *Under Western Eyes*, other than the letter in which Conrad outlined his intentions to Galsworthy, comes from Jessie's letter to David Meldrum, quoted at the beginning of this essay. Only a few days before this letter, Jessie wrote Pinker: "Only two hours before Conrad was taken ill he absolutely forbade me to touch the M. S. which he had arranged after a great deal of trouble."[51] Her comments in these letters have given rise to the "revision myth," a myth strongly developed by Baines, Davis, and Karl who several times refer to the "unrevised" condition of the novel during the early spring of 1910.[52] Conrad's 15 October 1911 letter to Galsworthy has further encouraged this view: "Revising while ill in bed, I am afraid I have struck out whole pages recklessly" (*LL*, II:136).[53] Both Conrad and his wife left impressions quite at odds with the facts. There are actually four important stages of revision of the novel. The first involves redefined intentions in January 1908, a point Karl has rightly identified as "a crucial month, when the story or novel could have gone in either direction, toward easy resolution or towards the kind of complication of narrative and narrator that Conrad considered to be his special mark" (Karl, 637). The second involves the actual composition of the manuscript as words, phrases, sentences, and paragraphs were recast, discarded, or added during the actual writing, the stage of revision so ably surveyed by Hay, Dalgarno, and Davis. The third and fourth stages deal with the typescript. Once Conrad received clean copy from Pinker's office, from his wife, or from Miss Hallowes, he meticulously revised, adding, deleting, or simply rewriting, first in black ink and pencil, then later in blue or indelible pencil — "later" is as long as twenty-seven months or as recently as two to three months — , and it is obviously to the indelible pencil set of revisions that both

Jessie and Conrad refer. In other words, the novel was apparently through the third state of revision before the 1910 breakdown and Jessie's letter to Meldrum. The "reckless striking" refers to the indelible pencil cancellations done in March-May 1910 when entire blocks and whole pages were struck, months during which Conrad's labors were assisted by those of Robert Garnett and of his own son Borys who, Conrad wrote Galsworthy, was "very tactful with his fractious father and really of great assistance in the arranging of MS. He put in order for me 600 pp all unnumbered and considerably shuffled working very methodically and with a quiet perseverance for an hour or so every morning."[54] In the same letter, he also told Galsworthy that Garnett "had been most friendly and wonderfully kind, volunteering to read over and correct the clean final copy. With three superimposed revisions there were a good many phrases without grammar and even without sense to be found in the rough typed copy."

Page after page establishes that the black-ink revisions came first, since blue pencil revisions often cancel them out. For example, "political saint"(TS, 95.15) was revised to "political hero" in black ink and then later cancelled entirely in indelible pencil. The sentence, "I am not a supernaturalist but what would you say if I were to tell you that I have been impelled"(TS I8.7-8), was first added in lead pencil, then all but the last four words were cancelled in indelible pencil. At times, recovering levels of composition from the typescript pages resembles archaeological excavation. A sentence in Packet D first read: "He made no sign but his arms folded sitting back rapidly, muttered" (TS, D1.8-9). This was revised to: "He folded his arms across his chest and muttered." At some point, Conrad added the clause: "he muttered contemptuously." And still later, he cancelled the first clause entirely, writing anew in indelible pencil:

"When I explained this to him he muttered contemptuously," a considerable evolution. Pages 215-27, 238-56, and 269-87, the major lengthy cancellations, were first carefully revised in black ink, indeed, honed sharply before being deleted by indelible slashes across each page. For instance, Victor Haldin emotionally hints his terrorist activities and plans to his sister. Natalia Haldin recalls for the narrator: "The only thing I can remember was when he said one evening to me in the garden of our house in the country that the destroyers must go first — the builders will come after. We had been having a discussion. He left me suddenly. He started for St. Petersburg next morning" (TS, 241.13-18). The fact that these cancellations are in the late indelible pencil stage should lay to rest speculations that Conrad deleted them in response to Galsworthy's 1908 criticism.

A full census of the revisions must be completed before any definitive statements can be made about their exact nature. Some revisions obviously show Conrad at his best; others are questionable. Examples involving the five major characters will give some idea of the nature of the "reckless cutting." Conrad further distanced Peter Ivanovitch from Leo Tolstoy, for example, when he struck "Ultimately he went into the barracks of an infantry regiment to preach brotherly love to soldiers" (TS, 205.2-4). Victor Haldin, we discover, was once more closely aligned with rational action. Natalia tells the narrator, "My brother was a reasonable being. He had formed a plan; he had resolved upon a line of action and I am sure that his plan included some provision for at least an attempt to escape. He was not a mere desperado" (TS, 310.5-8), or at least not until the blue pencil stroke cancelled the passage. Originally, the narrator had suffered at the hands of Peter Ivanovitch: "I don't think I would have called, since Peter Ivanovitch had somehow managed to rob me of perhaps my last illusion in life" (TS, 287.15-17), he tells us, before Conrad revised this sentence to "I don't think I should have called on her yet. My desire to keep her away from these people was a[s] strong as ever, but I had no illusions as to my power. I was but a Westerner. . . ." The narrator's perspective suddenly acquires pointed direction and an ironic sensibility. One might regret the deletion of the following insight into Razumov's perception of his situation: "a matter of life and death. But in reality it was an issue of greater moment because failure meant something worse than mere death to his imagination. He felt also that the contest was not equal for him; this feeling interpreted such an inconvertible truth that it was only extreme rage that kept him from giving way to despair. He rubbed stealthily the palms of his hands against his legs without lowering his gaze for a moment"(TS, 111.2-9).

Thus, far from having been hastily revised, *Under Western Eyes* experienced revision in both intermediate and final typescript (the black ink stage), and then a revision which probably *was* reckless and often ill-considered in the indelible pencil stage, which belongs to late spring, 1910. In May 1910, Conrad wrote Galsworthy, Henry Davray, and Rothenstein that revision had been completed.[55]

The sections of the Philadelphia typescript which are apparently first state (the last 349 pages) are quite close to the manuscript and show more extensive attention to the psychology of the characters than do the first three hundred pages. It should be noted that this section of the novel was heavily revised for the serial publication in *The English Review*.[56] The following example which pointedly underlines for Razumov the feminine powers which the novel both simultaneously satirizes and affirms was cancelled in the indelible pencil stages of revision after undergoing virtually no revision in either the manuscript or the typescript:

He was calmed by his self communion; that

> dread which had kept him for days from
> facing Miss Haldin, was gone. He felt
> nothing of it, perhaps simply for the reason
> that now he had a story to tell. It had been
> steeled for him; there was nothing to do
> but to have it over and done with. The fact
> that these were women he was going to meet
> did not trouble him especially. As a matter
> of fact he did not recognise women as
> women. There had been literally no feminine
> influence in his life. Women were human beings
> for him and nothing more, somewhat in the
> background, not to be thought of in any special
> way. He simply knew nothing of them in any
> relation, no woman had ever influenced a dream
> of his, taken up a moment of his time, or
> awakened any of his dormant feelings; no thought
> of woman had enriched his life by a touch of
> amenity, of colour, of reverie. It may be
> said that, in a manner, he had never seen a
> woman, for even Sophia Antonovna was a conspirator,
> a revolutionist, a dangerous person with whom he
> must be on his guard more than with anybody else —
> nothing more. (TS, R.9)

Razumov's world has indeed been a male one: in the orphanage, in the school, in the university, in the revolutionary circle. Other than the shadowy figures of his landlady and Prince K — 's haughty wife, Tekla, Sophia, and Natalia are the only women with whom he has come in contact for any noticeable period.

In general, we may say that Conrad often tended to overwrite, very often seeing revision as a process of tightening and compressing. In December 1909, he wrote Perceval Gibbon, "then with proper shortening carried all through the body of it (say five lines (on average) in every page) it will come out as [a] 150,000 word novel, reading yet swiftly enough.[57] Such a process is nowhere borne out by the typescript. There are many cancellations, corrections, and revisions which sharpen phrasing, focus theme, and adjust grammar. The deletions of most interest involve the narrator's comments, Razumov's understanding of relationships, descriptions of Madame de S— and the Château Borel revolutionaries, and the climactic encounter in which Razumov confesses to Natalia.

An indication of Conrad's deepening understanding of his material is glimpsed in the evolution of Razumov's discovery about betrayal. On 6 January 1908, Conrad outlined the first parts of "Razumov" to Galsworthy, noting that Part One was "done," the other "to do." The part yet to be done involved "The student Razumov meeting abroad the mother and sister of Haldin falls in love with that last, marries her and, after a time, confesses the part he played in the arrest of her brother" (*LL*, II:90–91). At this time Conrad had completed only the first chapter of the novel. Except for the marriage, these authorial intentions are fully realized at every stage in the composition, but not the nature of the discovery. Conrad continued his description: "the psychological developments leading to Razumov's betrayal of Haldin, to his confession of the fact to his wife and to the death of these people (brought about mainly by the resemblance of their child to the late Haldin), form the real subject of the story." At first, Conrad perceived a Razumov tortured by the betrayal of another human being. By mid-1908, he had transferred the resemblance to Haldin from a child to Natalia herself and dropped the idea of the marriage. In Packet B, for instance, the narrator, who could scarcely know, remembers: "As to the resemblance between brother and sister such resemblance unless so pronounced as to take in one or the other a grotesque aspect is the most elusive thing imaginable under the play of changing momentary expression, unless indeed the common moods of both persons are well known to the beholder" (TS, B1.15-20). Shortly after this, Natalia tells the narrator: "'You know people used to say our voices were at times alike. Mine is rather deep for a girl. He had listened to me; and what would he imagine the intentions of the sister of Victor Haldin to be?'"(TS, C4.21-5.1). By the time Conrad prepared final copy for the printer, he had internalized Razumov's sense of betrayal so deeply that Razumov was no longer betraying avatars of Haldin but had come fully to recognize that he had betrayed himself. Conrad early grasped the necessity of detailing the "psychological developments," but only as the text evolved in revision did he find a sufficient correlation. A child would have been melodramatic; Natalia would have been simply repetition; with a stroke of insight, Conrad saw that Razumov must intuit that she occupies the same innocent detachment he once did and that he has come knowingly and maliciously to play Haldin's role. This recognition necessitated a major rewriting of Razumov's confession. The central moment of insight originally read: "misery because the real truth is that in giving your brother up. It was myself that I have betrayed most basely. It was seeing you that I understood this. Most basely. And therefore perdition is my lot. There he stopped, shut the book and wrapped round it Natalia's veil he had carried off." Conrad brilliantly turned this passage into one of Razumov's key statements: "In giving Victor Haldin up, it was myself after all that I have betrayed most basely. You must believe me. You can't refuse to believe this. Most basely. It is through you that I came to feel this so deeply. Therefore it is they and not I who have the right on their side — the strength of invisible powers. So be it. Only don't be deceived Natalia Victorovna. I am not converted. Have I then the soul of a slave? No! I am independent — and therefore perdition is my lot. On these words he stopped writing, shut the book and wrapped round it the black veil he had carried off . . . " (TS, T.15.10-16.3). The admission of self-betrayal becomes a Munch-like moment of anguish, with Natalia becoming the instrument leading to his insight.

In short, then, this typescript enables us to understand the creative process of Conrad more precisely, to pinpoint the moment when key scenes in the novel took shape and under what circumstances, to wonder why Conrad at times made his text less particular, and to sense more closely why "the completion of *Under Western Eyes* marks the end of an era." [58] No one can regret that Conrad took the opportunity to cancel such lines as "It was a strange scene of a dumb maniac beating a corpse by the light of a lantern held by a man turned into stone" (TS, 44.14-15) and "Their silent immobility before each other resembled the self- forgetfulness of sorrow facing tragic enigma" (TS, K.6.3-5), and everyone can rejoice that Borys Conrad, Edward and Robert Garnett, Gabriel Wells, Richard S. Gimble, and others preserved this most crucial artifact. With the landmarks thus delineated more obviously, we can understand more fully why, on 28 June 1910, Conrad wrote Pinker, "I feel like a man returned from hell and look upon the very world of the living with dread." [59]

NOTES

I wish to express my thanks to the staff of the Rare Book Room of the Philadelphia Free Library and the New York Public Library for their assistance during my study of the typescript and related letters and to the National Endowment for the Humanities which provided assistance in the form of a Travel-to-Collections Grant, and to Deans Lawrence Graves, William B. Conroy, and Joe R. Goodin, who have supported my research on Conrad.

I owe a more substantial debt to my co-editor of the Cambridge edition of *Under Western Eyes*, Keith Carabine. Some of the conclusions concerning the dating of batches of the manuscript and packets of the typescript come from his work, and, refreshingly, we arrived at a number of identical conclusions concerning the typescript while working independently. I could not have wished for a more generous Conradian as a colleague in our work.

I also wish to thank Laurence Davies and Frederick R. Karl for giving me access to their transcriptions of the letters in the forthcoming Volume Four of the *Complete Letters*. Their generosity has enabled me to correct earlier printings of several of the letters, to date certain letters more precisely, and to check every letter cited in this paper.

[1] Richard S. Gimbel's note accompanying the typescript, for example, calls it a "M.S." or manuscript, though he then immediately calls the holograph revisions "manuscript additions."

[2] *The Edward Garnett Collection of Inscribed Books and Autograph Material by Joseph Conrad and W. H. Hudson* (New York: American Art Association, 1928), Item 73, p. 16.

[3] *Garnett Collection*, p. 17. The page reproduced is TS B1.

[4] *Complete Catalogue of the Library of John Quinn* (New York: The Anderson Galleries, 1924), p. 166, Lot 1781; *The Library of Jerome Kern* (New York: The Anderson Galleries, 1929), Part One, p. 92, Item 288. The prices are marked in the margins of the copies in Special Collections, Texas Tech University Library.

⁵ Daniel J. Levinson, *The Seasons of a Man's Life* (New York: Ballantine, 1979), p. 192; also see pp. 191, 197, 248.

⁶ Quoted by Emily Izsak Dalgarno, "*Under Western Eyes* and the Problems of Serial Publication," *RES*, 23 (1972), 431.

⁷ Letter of 6 January 1908, MS Forbes, also quoted by Frederick R. Karl in Karl, pp. 634-35. The discrepancy between Conrad's reference to "eleven novels" and my reference to *Under Western Eyes* as the "ninth novel" comes from counting or ignoring the collaborative volumes, *The Inheritors* (1901) and *Romance* (1903).

⁸ The letter continues: "As I've told you my mind runs very much on popularity just now. I would try to reach it not by sensationalism but by means of taking a widely discussed subject for the *text* of my novel. Apart from religious problems the public mind runs on questions of war and peace and labour. I mean war, peace, labour in general not any particular war or any particular form of labour trouble" (439-40).

⁹ The *Country Life, Daily News,* and *Daily Telegraph* items are quoted in Karl, pp. 626 and 648-49.

¹⁰ Letter of Sunday night, August 1908, quoted in Karl, p. 649. This and all subsequent letters of 1908–1910 are quoted with permission of Frederck R. Karl and Laurence Davies and are taken from the forthcoming Volume IV of the *Collected Letters.*

¹¹ Letter of 16 April 1909; quoted in Karl, p. 669. For Conrad's relationship with Pinker during these months, see Baines, 359-61.

¹² For discussions of continuous composition, see Emily K. Izsak [Dalgarno], "*Under Western Eyes* and the Problems of Serial Publication," *RES*, 23 (1972), 429, 434, and Baines, p. 347; for the possibility that Conrad withheld portions, see Dalgarno, p. 437; for consideration of Galsworthy's influence, see Roderick Davis, *Under Western Eyes*: "the most deeply meditated novel," *Conradiana*, 9 (1977), 62; for problems with the ending, see Dalgarno, pp. 431-32, and Davis, pp. 60-61; for discussions of the unrevised nature of the manuscript, see Davis, p. 62 and Karl, p. 682, who writes that "*Under Western Eyes,* of course,

remained unrevised." Karl is the source of one misrepresentation which has now widely entered Conrad scholarship. He commented that the first edition of *Under Western Eyes* is "about 30,000 words fewer than the serial text" (703). Zdzisław Najder, in *JCC* p. 574, repeats the error, as do Norman Page, *A Conrad Companion* (New York: St. Martin's Press, 1986), p. 106 and Cedric Watts's new biography, *Joseph Conrad: A Literary Life* (New York: St. Martin's Press, 1989), pp. 112–13. I hope that my "Conrad, *Under Western Eyes*, and the Mysteries of Revision," *RES*, 39 (1988), 231-44 has laid this scholarly ghost to rest by demonstrating that the serial and the first edition are the same length.

[13] See the Quinn Catalogue, pp. 185-87.

[14] Dalgarno, p. 429. The already mentioned Dalgarno and Davis items, along with Hay, 265-313, and Roderick Davis's unpublished dissertation, "Joseph Conrad's *Under Western Eyes*: A Genetic, Textual, and Critical Study" (Columbia University, 1973) constitute the major considerations of the *Under Western Eyes* manuscript.

[15] Kern Catalogue, p. 92.

[16] See H. Gilbert Kelley, "Bequest of Gabriel Wells," *Journal of the Rutgers University Library*, 10:2 (June 1947), 33-34.

[17] The typescript's existence became generally known in August 1980 during Donald W. Rude's worldwide census of Conrad manuscripts, typescripts, and unmarked and marked proofs. I studied the typescript first on microfilm during the fall of 1980 and the spring of 1981 and then at the Philadelphia Free Library in June 1981 and again in June 1984, thanks to a Travel-to-Collections Grant from the National Endowment for the Humanities.

[18] See Table Two for a full description of the typescript. Because the typescript pages are not numbered after page 313, I have referred to the lettered packets. Thus, an entry from Packet A, unnumbered page 6 would appear as TS, A6. At some point in the typescript's history, Packets A-H have been placed after I-T, undoubtedly in the packing of the document, a fact of no significance though the Philadelphia Free Library has kept the

packets in this reversed order. Several leaves have also been misplaced. H17 does follow from H16; R18 belongs in Packet T since it contains the text for 365.15-31; A1 now in Packet T belongs with Packet A because it contains the text for 158.14–159.6. H17 is most interesting, because it contains a very early state of the transition from Razumov's deafening to Mrs. Haldin's funeral. These pages simply appear to have been torn loose from the brads at some point.

[19] The "Original first typed copy of *Victory*" (Philadelphia Free Library) consists of thirteen bradded packets, which, beginning with Packet 5 are lettered A through G with Packets 12 and 13 being unlettered. This typescript, however, has consecutive pagination throughout.

[20] The two paragraphs are 366.27-367.8.

[21] ALS, Tuesday [8 April 1910], Bryn Mawr College Library, quoted by permissions of Leo M. Dolenski, Manuscripts Librarian and the Joseph Conrad Estate.

[22] ALS, [15 April 1910], Philadelphia Free Library, quoted by permission of the Rare Books Room, Philadelphia Free Library and the Joseph Conrad Estate.

[23] Letter of 17 May 1910, MS Forbes.

[24] The four stages in the creation of a work are (1) Preparation, (2) Incubation, (3) Illumination or Writing and (4) Verification or Revision and Editing. Quite obviously, stages two through four occur simultaneously in Conrad's habits of composition.

[25] See Karl, p. 635; also Dalgarno and Davis.

[26] See Karl, pp. 635 and 638, and Dalgarno, p. 431.

[27] Letter of May 1908. This and subsequent unpublished letters to Pinker are quoted, unless otherwise noted, with permissions of the Joseph Conrad Estate and the Henry W. and Albert A. Berg Collection, The New York Public Library, Astor, Lenox, and Tilden Foundation.

[28] Letter of Tuesday, 14 July 1908, Berg Collection.

[29] Letters of 30 September 1908 and 8 October 1908, Berg Collection.

[30] Letter of 13 October 1908, Berg Collection.

[31] Letter of 13 October 1908, Berg Collection. The chapter numbering may be momentarily confusing to those not familiar with the manuscript and the typescript. The divisions are clearly marked in both documents, especially in the typescript. The numbering runs thus: Chapter I (TS 1–36), II (37–104), III (105–66), IV (167–202), V (202–235), and VI (235–87). These breaks correspond to the existing breaks in the text.

[32] For a discussion of the preparation of the *Almayer's Folly* typescript, see David Leon Higdon and Floyd Eugene Eddleman, "The Typescript of Conrad's *Almayer's Folly*", *TSLL*, 18 (1976), 98-123.

[33] The notations to the typist appear on MS1, 11, 51, 71, 93, 100, 109, 127, 165, 172, 179, 231, 244, 254, 248, 280, 291, 298, 329, 330, 367, 388, 396, 404, 422, 423, 435, 457, 463, 487, 493, 512, 524, 554, 555, 584, 585, 593, 601, 650, 701, 714, and 729. The manuscript is cited with permission of the Beinecke Rare Book and Manuscript Library and the Joseph Conrad Estate.

[34] Letter of Monday, 1909, Berg Collection.

[35] MS 440-41, 447-48, 842, 899, and 1267A become TS 210-11, 214-15, G1, I1, and S1-2.

[36] In the following, deletions are in italics, and holograph additions are in brackets.

[37] Borys Conrad, *My Father: Joseph Conrad* (New York: Coward-McCann, 1970), p. 14.

[38] Letter of Tuesday, August 1908, Berg Collection .

[39] MS Berg, unpublished.

[40] I explored this aspect of the novel in a paper, "Joseph Conrad and the Shapes of Time," which I delivered at the inaugural symposium of the Scandinavian Joseph Conrad Society, 23 September 1988,

[41] MS Berg, unpublished.

[42] MS Berg and MS Darmouth, Schwab, unpublished.

[43] MS Texas, unpublished.

[44] These dates have posed something of a mystery for Conradians over the years, and arguments have developed as to whether they are for 1908 or 1909. They are clearly 1909 dates, but see Dalgarno, 432 and Karl, p. 670.

[45] MS Berg, unpublished.

[46] MS Forbes, see *LL*, II, 90. There may be a dating problem with the two letters, separated as they are by only five days. Conrd's letters alludes to the intermediate typescript ("the very many pages now destroyed" and hints of the changing conceptions.

[47] See Keith Carabine, "'The Secret Sharer': A Note on the Dates of Its Composition," *Conradiana*, 19 (1987), 209-13.

[48] Quoted in *TTL*, p. 658.

[49] Letter of Monday, August 1909, Berg Collection.

[50] See the Tables for the page counts. These are in line with Conrad's general habit of sending packets of 20 to 30 pages of manuscript.

[51] Letter of 3 February 1910, Berg Collection.

[52] See Baines, pp. 372-73, and *TTL*, p. 682.

[53] For a printing of one of the three major cuts and a discussion of its significance, see David Leon Higdon and Robert F. Sheard, "Conrad's 'Unkindest Cut': The Canceled Scenes in *Under Western Eyes*," *Conradiana*, 19 (1987), 167-81.

[54] Letter of 17 May 1910. MS Forbes.

[55] Letter of 3 May 1910 to Davray, Humanities Research Center, University of Texas at Austin.

[56] See my "Conrad, *Under Western Eyes*, and the Mysteries of Revision." *RES*, 49 (1988), 231-44.

[57] Quoted in Dalgarno, p. 433.

[58] *TTL*, p. 678.

[59] Letter 28 June 1910, Humanities Research Center, University of Texas at Austin.

TABLE ONE
Page Correlation of British Edition, Typescript, Manuscript

Kent Edition	Typescript	Manuscript
Part First		
3.03-7.4	1-7	1-16
(i) 7.5-24.13	(I) 7-36	17-70
(ii) 24.14-66.30	(II) 37-104	71-215
(iii) 66.31-99.33	(III)105-166	216-338
(97)	(166)	(338)
Part Second		
(i) 100.01-118.21	(IV) 167-202	339-418
(ii) 118.22-131.19	(V) 202-235	418-498
(iii) 131.20-140.23	(VI) 235-287	498-618
(iv) 140.24-182.12	(VII) 287-C13	619-758
(v) 182.13-197.18	C13-D24	758-806
(97)	(223)	(468)
Part Third		
(i) 198.01-214.30	E1-G15	807-861
(ii) 214.31-237.30	G15-I34	861-942
(iii) 237.31-264.29	I34-K19	942-1037
(iv) 264.30-292.05	K19-M19	1037-1123
(95)	(243)	(317)
Part [Fourth]		
(i) 293.01-316.02	M19-O25	1123-1188
(ii) 316.03-335.24	O25-Q18	1188-1243
(iii) 335.25-356.27	Q18-T5	1243-1339
(iv) 356.28-371.29	T5-[X]2	1340-1343
[v] 371.30-382.19	[X]2-[X]25	1344-1351
(90)	(211)	(228)
TOTALS		
380 pages	843 pages	1351 pages

TABLE TWO
Philadelphia Free Library Typescript of *Under Western Eyes*
Description

Packet	Leaves	Pages	Date	Spacing	Type Color	Lines	Pages Without/With Revision	Watermarking
[1]	55	55	None	Double	Purple	1082	10/45	Oceana Superfine
[2]	60	60	None	Double	Purple	1114	18/42	Oceana Superfine
[3]	87	87	None	Double	Purple	1611	9/78	Oceana Superfine (116–51, 157–202), Excelsior Superfine (152–306)
[4]	32	32	None	Double	Purple	607	6/26	Oceana Superfine
[5]	78	78	None	Double	Purple, Black	1603	10/68	Oceana Superfine (236–88, 308–13), Excelsior Superfine (289–306), No Watermark (307)
A	14	14	None	Double	Purple, Blue	311	1/13	Oceana Superfine
B	12	12	1-21-10	Double	Blue	278	2/10	Oceana Superfine
C	27	27	1-21-10	Double (C1-14) Triple (C15-27)	Blue	477	7/20	Oceana Superfine
D	24	24	2-10	Triple	Blue	304	4/20	Oceana Superfine

E	10	12	None	Triple	Blue	115	0/9 + holograph	Oceana Superfine (E1-E6, E8-E10), Rock Leigh Mill (E7)
F	14	14	None	Triple	Blue	183	0/14	Oceana Superfine
G	27	27	None	Triple	Blue	360	1/26	Oceana Superfine
H	16	16	None	Triple	Blue	207	2/14	No Watermark
I	36	36	None	Triple	Blue	459	2/34	No Watermark
J	51	51	9-24,10-2	Triple	Blue	641	8/43	No Watermark
K	26	26	10-16	Triple	Blue	326	6/20	No Watermark
L	42	42	10-29	Triple	Blue	547	14/28	No Watermark
M	22	22	11-12,11-19	Triple	Blue	286	6/16	No Watermark
N	29	29	None	Triple	Blue	376	0/29	No Watermark
O	28	28	11-27	Triple	Blue	363	0/28	No Watermark
P	26	26	12-4	Triple	Blue	336	5/21	No Watermark
Q	21	21	12-21	Triple	Blue	273	4/17	No Watermark
R	18	18	1-15-10	Triple	Blue	234	1/17	No Watermark
S	30	30	1-27-10	Triple	Blue	385	9/21	No Watermark
T	31	31	1-21-10	Triple	Blue	415	0/31	No Watermark (T–1T–30), Excelsior Superfine (T31)
[X]	25	25	None	Holograph	Lead pencil		0/25	Fine Commercial

Oddities remarked: 37-44 were once numbered A2-H2, surely another indication of the presence of an intermediate typescript; 223-224 are a combined page; 120-22, 24-34 were once numbered 1-3, 4-13. The January-February 1910 dates on Packets B-D probably refer to a retyping.

Under Western Eyes
And the Missing Center

Eloise Knapp Hay

At the heart of *Under Western Eyes* there is one of those missing elements that show Conrad to "glory in a gap." The phrase is Henry James's, and he meant it as a compliment. He was comparing Conrad with Bennett and Lawrence, whose novels (James said) "smell of the real" yet lack the "mysteries" of method through which alone art can convey the thickness and complexity of the real.[1] James himself was no mean glorier in the narrative gap. He had only to maximize what he inherited from his beloved Hawthorne — in *The Blithedale Romance*, for instance — or from his friend Browning. In 1890 Ernest Dowson wrote of Browning: "The subtility, the tact of omission, the Morbidezza! 'My Last Duchess', par exemple, is pure Henry James ...."[2]

The genealogy of this "tact of omission" concerns me less, however, than the way Conrad employs it in *Under Western Eyes*. James knew his Conrad well when he said the "gap" served him in creating a narrative "fusion between what we are to know and that prodigy of our knowing which is ever half the very beauty of the atmosphere of authenticity."[3] In *Under Western Eyes* the gap exists as a

121

deliberately missing point of view that is needed if "that prodigy of our knowing" is to come about.

The missing point of view in this case is not simply the implied author's viewpoint, for in *Under Western Eyes* there are several such viewpoints, some pro others contra the "Western eyes." The implied Conrad who was a naturalized British citizen sees quite differently from the implied Conrad who was an Eastern European. The implied author whose voice seems audible in the liberal conservative Razumov's words is often contradicted by the implied author deliberately speaking through the revolutionists Haldin and his sister, longing for freedom at any cost. All three of these Russians are contradicted from time to time by the implied Conrad who speaks persuasively through the conservative narrator, an Englishman. There are thus multiple authorities in the novel, all with urgent appeals — more than in any other novel I know. The reader is made to sit as a jury of twelve deciding the case, in the end finding that an unseen, inaudible judge will have the last word. The voice of this final judge (invented by Conrad as are the audible voices) is heard only through its conspicuous absence.

As Conrad wrote in letters between 1908 and 1911, then later in the Author's Note (1920), because of "the peculiar experience of [his] race [i.e., nationality] and family," his personal views had to be subjected to "earnest meditation" and then converted into "general truth," or "general knowledge" for the sake of achieving a view of "scrupulous impartiality" in the novel. It pleased him greatly to learn in the year of the Bolshevik Revolution "that the book had found universal recognition in Russia,"[4] the hub of his worst phobias, thus proving his success in achieving the "very detachment" that made the novel, ironically, a failure in England. If he had made the book's central heartbeat more audible, he thought, it would have had a more immediate impact in the narrator's England (*UWE*, vi–viii).

Everything in the novel is filtered through the English narrator, who gradually undercuts his own credibility, at first through disclaimers about his comprehension and later through miscomprehensions that he does not acknowledge in his powers of observation. The reader is finally at a loss to find any truth figure, such as we can find in other Conrad novels where the narrator is plainly to be trusted (however fallible) — in *Lord Jim* and "The Secret Sharer," for instance. *Under Western Eyes* is more like *Heart of Darkness* in that both narratives end up outmaneuvering and undermining even their most observant and sympathetic speakers. If Marlow, returning from Africa, has to lie to everyone, it is because of his own complicities in "the civilizing work" going forward in the Congo (*LBM*; 37, Hay 134–52). Marlow has identified himself with the great explorers, adventurers, and idea men whose notions of progress have ended in genocide. The English teacher in *Under Western Eyes* has no such repressed reasons for retelling Razumov's story as Marlow has in uneasily retelling Kurtz's — and his own — , but we may well ask if the English teacher has any reasons at all. As a man who holds no brief for his story's hero, Razumov, this narrator contrasts even more strikingly with the narrators of "The Secret Sharer" and *Lord Jim*. (Marlow's concluding question in the latter, "Was I so very wrong after all?", can only be answered in the negative, thus confirming the validity of his long, intense inquiry about Jim's ability to remain "true.")

In both *Heart of Darkness* and *Under Western Eyes*, by contrast, the narrators end by reviling the central figures of their narratives, making the reader look elsewhere than to these men for the narrators' motives in telling their stories. Both narrators protest too much about their nation's

— England's — immunity to the infamous events they un-
fold: *cosas de Russia* (as Conrad called them) and Africa.
Conrad could not expose the crimes in Russia, however,
the way he had represented the horrors in Africa. As he declared in letters to Garnett and Galsworthy while writing
Under Western Eyes and in the Author's Note nine years after finishing it, he felt honor-bound to treat the Russians as
sympathetically as justice and truth demanded, somehow
overcoming the disgust and trauma induced by the first six-
teen years of his life. His personal hostility to Russia stood
in his mind much as his personal attachment to England
had stood when he wrote *Heart of Darkness*, as a silencer to
his Polish protests against the two nations that had claimed
his allegiance — Russia by force of conquest and England as
the foster homeland that saved him from carrying a Russian
passport. It required no effort to treat England sympathetically; the effort was rather to keep harsh feelings about
British imperialism under wraps, or at least under control.
In the case of Russia, at the other extreme, it was control over feelings in which sympathy failed altogether that
was needed. What better control could he find for *Under
Western Eyes* than to counterpose an English narrator with
whom his sympathies were mixed rather than simple (one
whose point of view would admit suspicion) against the
Russian czarists and revolutionists? Conrad's object being
to show the "senseless desperation provoked by senseless
tyranny" in these Russian antagonists (*UWE*, viii), the readers' "sense" must be their own after cool reflection on the
contrary appeals of "East" and "West" that underlie the
novel's argument. And it is this central position, the point
of view from which the whole novel must be viewed, that
is missing, left unstated, in the novel.

Like the impartial judge Conrad wished to be, he relied
on his jury, his readers, to supply this central viewpoint.

The difficulties of implanting such a space, authoritative but not authorial, immanent yet also transcendent (like Flaubert's "God of creation, everywhere felt and nowhere seen") undoubtedly played a large part in the mental breakdown Conrad suffered in 1910 while finishing the novel. The chief cost to his psychic strength, however, appears to have been the mouthpiece of the novel, the English narrator, whose comments underwent most revision in the manuscript. The old teacher, like Marlow in Africa though even more distant from Conrad than Marlow, has to convey more truth than he is able to seize upon himself, including evidence that favors the Russians which he cannot interpret because of his narrowly Western bias. The novel's effect is finally to show the failure of any standpoint that is not both an insider's (Russian) and also an outsider's simultaneously.

David Smith has suggested that this might well have been Conrad's own position since he was born a Russian citizen who was Polish.[5] I would add only that such an awkward position might have *prevented* an "objective" point of view if Conrad had not exerted himself exhaustingly to counterbalance it. The novel's nameless English narrator provides the counterweight by being doubly an outsider — a foreigner among the Russians and also among the "Westerners" by virtue of his birth in Russia to parents of British citizenship. This narrator is thus, like Conrad, born in "Russia," but unlike Conrad he never had to carry a Russian passport, nor does he concern himself with Russia's subject peoples, or wonder particularly about the meaning of "Western eyes." These matters, so vital to Conrad, are of no importance to the English narrator.

The structure of the novel is such that the reader is hardly aware of having a problem with the narrator's point of view for 100 pages, or until Part Second when the old

teacher stops summarizing Razumov's diary and begins recalling his own role in the story — some time before he met
Razumov in Geneva. The shift, he acknowledges, is abrupt
because (he pleads) "this is not a work of imagination"
and he "would not even invent a transition," since "artlessness" is a virtue when he is "strong in the sincerity of
[his] purpose" (100). He has named this purpose somewhat
earlier: his "task" is to render "the moral conditions ruling
over a large portion of this earth's surface" — by which he
means, of course, among the Russian people. At that point
he gave us as much of a clue as he will ever give concerning what he thinks of those "moral conditions." They can
be understood, he had said, only when "some key-word is
found; a word that could stand at the back of all the words
covering the pages" and "help the moral discovery which
should be the object of every tale." This word, which "per-
sists in creeping under [his account] . . . is no other word
than 'cynicism'" (67). By the end of the novel, being given
no more reason than this for the Englishman's writing, we
must decide for ourselves whether all the Russians are cyn-
ical or only some and whether this narrator is a competent
judge. It gradually dawns on us that he cannot distinguish
one cynic from another but is, perhaps, tarring all Russians
with the same brush while whitewashing all "Westerners."

In the revised, or published, versions of *Under Western
Eyes* these "Western eyes" receive no critical examination.
Since the narrator specifies that his record is aimed at readers only in "the West of Europe" (25), it is unnecessary for
him to accommodate other readers, and he stuffily assumes
there will be no different opinions from his even among the
French and Germans, to say nothing of his fellow English-
men. Recalling, however, that in *Lord Jim* — where the
reader's judgment was equally open to dispute — Marlow
almost obsessively tested his views against both his listeners

and other Western Europeans like Brierly, the French Lieu-
tenant, and Stein, one stops to think. The teacher's English
eyesight goes uncorrected by the Russians or anyone else in
the novel, and this is strange in view of Conrad's many assertions that the point of view he adopted as an English
novelist was never transparent (e.g., *CL*, II:157, *CPB*, 240).

Once the Englishman's view of events takes over the
narrative, in Parts Second through Four of the novel, the
contrast between his view and Razumov's, which governed
Part First, is so great that early readers of the novel suspected Conrad of losing imaginative control. Replying to
one such reader, Olive Garnett, Conrad insisted to the
contrary that control was just what the English narrator had provided. Defending this dullish narrator, he said
the novel "had to be a performance on one string. It had
to be. You may think such self-imposed limitation a very
stupid thing. But something of the kind must be done or
else novel-writing becomes a mere debauch of the imagination"(*LG*, 234). Evidently Dostoevsky stood principally in
his mind at the time as this sort of novelist. *Under Western
Eyes* is generally recognized as in many ways an answer
to, a rewriting of, *Crime and Punishment*, and while at
work on it Conrad spoke forcefully of his wish to maintain
"self-possession" against a Dostoevskian "surrender . . . to
occult and irresponsible powers." In the same thinly veiled
comparison between his work and the Russian's, he con-
ceded that his concern for control might be said to set
his own novels at a level below "the highest achievement"
of the other if the criterion were "command over laughter
and tears" (*APR*, xvi–xvii). Yet here again, as in direct comments on *Under Western Eyes*, Conrad insists that appeal
to laughter and tears is less important than the imaginative
expression of "general truth," since "truth alone is the jus-
tification of any fiction" that lays a claim to art ("Author's

Note," vii–viii). Writing Garnett again some six months later, he accused Dostoevsky's novels of indulging in imaginative debauchery, "like some fierce mouthings from prehistoric ages" (*LG*, 240).

A fundamental difference distinguishing *Under Western Eyes* from *Crime and Punishment*, then, is the deliberately introduced control of a narrator who describes himself as alien to the Russian subject matter of his narrative. Frank Kermode rather hyperbolically noted the difference when he said that *Under Western Eyes* "does not simply encode a message from an author," as most other novels do; it "asserts the fallibility of all that it seems to assert."[6] Paradoxically, the much discussed polyphony of Dostoevsky's novels in no way disguises the author's encoded messages; whereas Conrad's "one string" narrator — especially in *Under Western Eyes* — encodes them to a point (the novel's missing center) where the message disappears and can be composed only by the reader. "Dialogism" such as we note in Raskolnikov's conversations with Marmeladov's family (including Sonya) or Luzhin's with Lebeziatnikov are brilliantly "heteroglossal" in their revelations of human nature in all its diversity, yet they tend invariably to the single, clear message of Dostoevsky's conclusion — that only through Christian hope and charity can depravity's despair, epitomized in Svidrigailov and socially diffused through such "lice" as Luzhin and the old pawnbroker, be combatted. Dostoevsky's novel is undoubtedly more ambitious than Conrad's, which only diagnoses the "senseless desperation provoked by senseless tyranny" in Russian life and character. *Crime and Punishment* not only diagnoses the sickness of soul and political consequences thereof throughout Russian society, but it also prescribes their cure. *Under Western Eyes* obliquely examines this sickness of soul, yet finds it as much in the beholder, the "Western eyes" of the narrator, as in the Russians under his observation. But this remains to be examined.

II

A sensitive reading of Conrad's novel demands that we measure first the distance between the narrator's point of view and the Russians', then the distance between our point of view and his if we are not to end with the unsatisfactory conclusion of a novel that implies the fallibility of all that it seems to assert. The English narrator's *close sympathy* with Razumov, oddly enough, impresses us first — throughout Part First — despite his recurrent claims to incomprehension of conditions in Russia and in Razumov's psychology. While he is transmitting the diary account of Razumov's situation when Haldin's intrusion changed everything, the narrator paradoxically subordinates "Western" thinking to Razumov's interior life — by dint of focusing on the series of Razumov's dramatic encounters: with Haldin, with Ziemianitch, with Prince K—, and with Mikulin. The narrator's attention to the diary account is so close that his disclaimers of understanding hardly do more than remind readers that we are safe in our "Western world" from the terror, loneliness, and desperation that provoke Razumov's deeply human yet terrible betrayal of Haldin. If the narrator had continued this intimate association between the diary's account and his own, we should never be drawn to doubt his interpretation of it, despite certain dubious comments that we recall later as weakening our confidence in his report. (I shall return to these later in considering the distance that finally determines our need to find another "center" for the novel than the one he provides.)

The Englishman's decision in Part Second to shift his narrative to his own story, his life in Geneva among the Russians of "la petite Russie" and his friendship with Haldin's sister and mother, has a number of effects on his tale, chief among them being his complete detachment from the man, Razumov, whose "eyes" were the truest center of the novel up to this point. Conrad's decision to "glory in a gap" was never more pronounced, and one would give much to know what James thought of this narrative leap if he read the novel. Garnett apparently interpreted the break from Razumov's interior story as evidence of Conrad's Polish callousness or want of sympathy with his subject, but ultimately the gap affects us as callousness on the narrator's part alone. As we noted, he pleads "artlessness" and inability to "invent a transition" as he begins Part Second; yet here is persuasive evidence that he is as little concerned for his readers' feelings as he is for Razumov's. From the narrator's point of view, it is just time to tell us how he came to know Razumov in Geneva. The gap and consequent severance of his concern for Razumov can hardly be explained either as providing suspense (What has become of Razumov?) or as showing how alienated Razumov has become from everyone, including the reader, now that he has been forced to serve as a police spy. Both effects would have been achieved as well by continuing to summarize the diary. Conrad evidently wished, however, to dramatize *the old Englishman's* detachment from Razumov at this point.

Readers who thought they were reading Razumov's story begin here to recognize that the narrator thinks otherwise — thinks that Razumov is merely an illustration of the judgment that right-thinking Westerners must reach concerning Russians in general. There is more than a fine line between seeing Razumov (or any man) as an end in himself and seeing him primarily as representative of some human condition the way the teacher does. Something prevents him from concentrating on Razumov. The Englishman gives out that it was his attachment to Natalia Haldin that determined his chill toward Razumov in the last two-thirds of his story, leading many readers to conclude that the dry old bachelor is in love with her unbeknownst to himself. We doubt finally that he could care sufficiently for anyone to be a lover. In any case, the narrator of *Under Western Eyes* thinks stereotypically, a flaw Conrad claimed he had to remove surgically from his own thinking while writing the novel. (Changing the narrative's title from the original *Razumov*, as he did after finishing the novel, made clear the Englishman's stress on his own "eyes" rather than the centrality of Razumov as hero.) Conrad uses the narrator's blindness to his mental block against Russians as the main instrument in creating what I call the missing center of the novel.

We could have noted even in Part First the Englishman's tendency to seal himself off from his living subjects, or rather to think of them as sealed off from him. He began his story by admitting his disregard for *words*, which "as is well known" (he says dubiously) "are the foes of reality" (3). In this, as almost everywhere else, he is quite opposite to Marlow telling the story of Lord Jim (so similar to Razumov, and perhaps deliberately so on Conrad's part). Jim's Marlow had said, "Frankly, it is not my words that I mistrust but your minds" (*LJ*, 225). Ignoring for the moment the English teacher's unwarranted trust of our minds, his mistrust of words must seem quirky in one who makes his living by them. But surely that is the point — he distrusts words the way a gambler distrusts cards, capitalizing on humanity's confidence in them. He is not a teacher of history or seamanship (which Conrad would have seen as constituting truths) but only of languages, the stuff from which truths can be unmade as easily as made. He is virtually a self-caricature of Conrad.

Of course the narrator cons no one but himself. He offers a good many solid and persuasive, even wordy, judgments. We recognize his absolute authority in Part First when he comments on Razumov's peculiarly Russian dilemma as an ambitious thinker in a land where thought itself is dangerous. The Englishman's chief anxiety about words results, furthermore, from his long experience of Russia and Russians, a people famously more expressive and voluble than the ordinary English, as he points out. Yet it is just that expressiveness and volubility we miss when the narrator interrupts his transmission of the diary. Notwithstanding his occasionally penetrating insights, the reader is distinctly inclined to prefer Razumov's own expression — filtered though it usually is — to the narrator's, and we miss Razumov's voice almost painfully when it is cut off. As Albert Guerard observed long ago, "The narrator's . . . obtuseness is one of the great sources of [the novel's] created sympathy for the damned."[7]

Another fact of the Englishman's life that distances him from the Russians is his voluntary exile from England, his homeland (as he queerly assumes though he has never lived there for long apparently). The Russians are exiles in Geneva by force of terrible circumstances; he by choice. When Natalia speaks longingly of a day when Russians will no longer live in exile but will achieve at home a solidarity better than any known so far in Western democracies, the narrator claims not to understand her. He defends democracy and majority rule in words that belie his dour feelings about Geneva (the perfect democracy embodied in the novel) and, we might add, in words that belie Conrad's own doubts about democracy (e.g. to Cunninghame Graham [*CL*, II:158] and later in "Autocracy and War" [*NLL*, 107]).

Natalia's thought is anything but incomprehensible (as the narrator insists it is) when she says, "We Russians shall find some better form of national freedom than an artificial conflict of parties — which is wrong because it is a conflict and contemptible because it is artificial." The Englishman answers, "I haven't understood — I won't say a single word; I've understood all the words .... But what can be this era of disembodied concord you are looking forward to? . . . The most idealistic conceptions of love and forbearance must be clothed in flesh as it were before they can be made understandable"(106). Not long after writing this Burkean passage, Conrad himself in one of his essays takes Natalia's stand. He argues in support of Poland as "a spiritual entity" and he bases his faith on "the strength of its ideals" despite its lack of fleshly existence outside Russia.[8] Indeed throughout his own exile in England, Conrad was closer to sharing Natalia's position than her English teacher's, at least in respect to national sentiment.

The narrator of *Under Western Eyes* has no such reasons for living outside his homeland as Conrad had. Born of English parents voluntarily residing in Russia, the narrator has inexplicably chosen not to go home again to England. In pursuit of his teaching languages, he has lived for the past twenty years in Geneva (188), "the passionless abode of democratic liberty," as he calls it (357), but no one in the novel is so passionless as he is. It is perhaps one of Conrad's little jokes that the narrator fantasizes about England's immunity to extremist politics even while he bemoans the absence of political excitement in Geneva. During the two decades the narrator has lived away from England (roughly 1885–1905), London — like most European capitals — took terrorist threats (and actual outrages) against officialdom very seriously, as witness *The Secret Agent*.

Nevertheless the Englishman insists, "To us Europeans of the West, all ideas of political plots and conspiracies seem childish, crude inventions for the theatre or a novel" (109). It is clearly his generally complacent and dull neutrality (like Geneva's) that makes him acceptable to the otherwise self-cloistering Russian community. Only Razumov dislikes the old man, but Razumov "feels rather more keenly" than the other Russians, as the Author's Note tells us. It also tells us that "feeling" rather than "thinking" governs the novel's course of action (viii–ix), suggesting that we place more of our trust in the passionate Razumov than in the tepid narrator.

Thus in many respects Razumov and the narrator are opposites as well as supplements, and some readers like David Leon Higdon have suggested they may be intended as alter egos. They both think of themselves as "professors" (potentially in Razumov's case); both appear as liberal conservatives, defending political evolution against violent revolutionaries; and Razumov's tragedy hinges on his appearing to fellow students as a "regular Englishman" in his cool reticence and "philosophical scepticism" (21–22). All of Conrad's major fiction represents the main characters as similarly juxtaposed with a stranger-reflector, locked unexpectedly into close relationship with at least one other figure, whether in an undesired "partnership" like Marlow's with Kurtz, in a sympathetic relationship that is relentlessly scrutinized, like Marlow's with Jim, or in one that is unconsciously acted out, like Nostromo's shadowing of Charles Gould in his obsession with the silver ingots.

Similar alter egos emerge constantly in the Romantic tradition of which Conrad was so much a part, from Godwin's *Caleb Williams* (1794) and Poe's "William Wilson" (1839) through the strange twinnings in Dickens and

Twain (to mention Anglo-American fiction alone). These Romantic doublings recall the mystery stressed by Friedrich Schlegel at the end of the 18th century when he said: "Often one cannot help thinking that two spirits should reunite as two halves that have been separated . . . it is only together that they become all that they can be . . . . All that is lacking in one . . . is found in the other."[9] Such might be said of the relation Razumov as diarist bears to the English recorder of his story. Though Razumov's psychological "twinning" with Haldin is the more essential relationship analyzed in *Under Western Eyes*, it is not the first of Conrad's novels to explore multiple doublings in the same narrative (witness Jim and Brierly, Jim and Brown as subnarrators and self-reflectors). The narrator of "The Secret Sharer," closest of all in provenance to *Under Western Eyes*, is a double not only explicitly of his fellow narrator Leggatt but also implicitly the double of his opposite, the despicable Captain Archbold.

Conrad's manuscript revisions show that the narrator of *Under Western Eyes* was originally conceived as even closer to Razumov in his point of view. Keith Carabine finds that the revisions downplaying the narrator's persuasiveness in effect strengthen Razumov's authority while diminishing the narrator's ("Behind the Veil"), and Higdon suggests that Conrad was careful to pare down "parallels between the narrator and Razumov . . . perhaps in a move to make his narrator more limited, less perceptive, more self-deluded about his true attraction to Razumov's story."[10] Undeniably the corrections make the narrator more limited and less perceptive, but neither early nor late in the composition of the novel do I see signs of his "attraction to Razumov's story" — an attraction based on identification with his subject such as we find, for instance, in the narrators telling the stories of Leggatt, Jim, and Kurtz.

Both the novel and its manuscript versions indicate that the Englishman was from the start to be unconsciously as well as consciously scandalized no less by Razumov himself — by his illogicality and mysticism as well as his prolixity — than by the dilemma into which he is thrown. To make this dull, half-perceptive narrator into someone worth reading, a believable Englishman whose Western mentality his readers would share up to a certain point but no farther — this was Conrad's evident plan. The Englishman must also be at least sympathetic enough to Natalia Haldin for her to place some confidence in him, and ultimately for her to entrust Razumov's diary to his keeping, thus disposing of it to someone likely to remain detached. These considerations are all we need to account for the highly conditional rapport between him and everyone else in the story he tells.

He is a cautious, fussy old bachelor whose ambivalence toward Natalia points to another parallel with Razumov — again with a huge difference. She is perhaps a surrogate for the daughter/wife missing in the narrator's life. One increasingly notes his shrinking from attachments that Razumov hungers for, and the narrator's relief, or at least inexplicable approval, when Natalia returns to Russia in the end, as he has advised her to do (372). In the novel's final version, he is still more self-isolating than in the first draft. There he described correspondence with an English niece who had moved to Canada. He scornfully criticized the cold materialism of her life in the Western hemisphere and her childless marriage after contracting with her husband to remain absolutely free in their partnership. Presumably Conrad cut out these references to the New World for many reasons: not only to shorten the novel and avoid alienating American readers but also to allow the narrator no close relatives and above all to emphasize the narrow-

ness of his idea of "the West." In the end his references
are only to "us Europeans," giving American readers other
reasons to question his judgments.

Still, what finally most displays his deficiencies are
his inhibitions against showing emotion, or sharing any of
the passions expressed in the story he is telling. Conrad
has this Englishman be the bearer of the tragic news of
Victor Haldin's death to Natalia and her mother. When
he informed them, he tells us, his sympathy was rendered
"uncertain" by Haldin's associations with "bombs and gal-
lows," and he was "grateful to Miss Haldin for not embar-
rassing [him] by an outward display of deep feeling"(112).
He then left the bereaved women with a perfunctory remark, unable to offer them a word of consolation. Natalia
quite justly turns her back on him and refuses his daily calls
for two weeks. Meanwhile he continues to find her and her
mother's reactions mysterious, hiding his discomfort behind
his belief, as he says, that "modes of feeling" differ from nation to nation, and such feelings as Natalia's are a terrible
obstacle for "our complex Western natures"(116-7).

In the end he calls Razumov's unburdening of his guilty
secret to Natalia an "atrocious confession," as though it is
a breach of etiquette or an offense against good taste (355,
375). Razumov's reaction is exactly right when he wakes up
to the Englishman's presence: "How did this old man come
here?"(355). This narrator has none of Marlow's sympathy
with the guilty man's truth and courage, which is what
the reader feels most in Razumov's case, as in Leggatt's or
Jim's. And just when we think the narrator may have risen
to an adequate sympathy (for he says "Something dimmed
my eyes" and we think "Tears?"), we learn instead that it
was the old man's horrified rage. He says, "That miserable
wretch has carried off your veil!"(356), as though the petty
theft were the real climax of the confession.

By now we know why this man can bear to live indefinitely alone in the city he calls "passionless," a city "tendering the same indifferent hospitality to tourists . . . and to international conspirators of every shade" (357). In that first quarter of the twentieth century Geneva may have been the only perfectly safe city in the world, but this last remark is made by the narrator impassively while describing the hours of Razumov's tormented confessions, hours following which there will be no possible hospitality for Razumov in Geneva. By now, furthermore, we must feel that the Englishman's motives in presenting Razumov's diary are both obscure and inconsistent — again in extreme contrast to what Razumov's motives were in writing *his* record. If, as most readers have assumed, the narrator's intentions are the same as Conrad's, described in the Author's Note, we cannot account for Conrad's very different statements there about Razumov: "I don't think that in his distraction he is ever monstrous" (ix). An implied comparison with Dostoevsky's Raskolnikov is likely in the Note, but the English narrator of the novel treats Razumov as if he were just such a murderer and a molester of women to boot. Disgusted as he is with Razumov after their last encounter, we wonder why he doesn't throw the diary away.

He accepts the diary from Natalia only because she wants to get rid of it without destroying it. She clearly reveres the desire for truth it represents, and she has to resist her love for its author even after learning about his part in her brother's execution. As the novel ends, while the narrator disengages himself from further concern for any of the Russians, the emptiness of his life and the inadequacy of his judgment appear dramatically. Of the man whose story so gripped us in Part First, now crippled and ruined, the narrator says, "Personally, I never went near him: I never saw him again, after the awful evening when I stood by, a watchful but ignored spectator of his scene with Miss Haldin"(377). Two pages later he says how surprised he is that the revolutionaries — who had so much more reason to despise Razumov than he has — regularly visit their fellow Russian, living (and dying) back in the heart of his homeland.

At this point we also glimpse a change in Razumov that would perhaps require comment if the narrator had sufficient interest in him. Sophia Antonovna reveals that Razumov, the formerly sceptical "regular Englishman" who remained so incommunicative in his student days, now welcomes the revolutionaries and is honored by them. As she says, "He has ideas .... He talks well, too"(379). The news may call to mind the narrator's opinion that words are "the great foes of reality"(3), but one can't help feeling that Razumov's gain in fellowship is more of a compliment to the Russian character than the narrator's arch silence is any advantage to him, however much this last news of Razumov may feed his belief in the "cynicism" of Russians.

In the end the narrator refuses comment also on Sophia Antonovna's cryptic accounts of the last days of Councillor Mikulin, Nikita, and Peter Ivanovitch. He appears just to abandon the effort, leaving us more in the dark than the most ambiguous narratives of Hawthorne, Melville, or James. If we recall for instance *The Turn of the Screw*, the narrating governess at least offered us two possible readings of a complete story. Either the evil ghosts of Quint and Miss Jessel did try to possess the children or the governess was predisposed to see them by virtue of her religious upbringing and romantic sensibility. The two readings are not in fact incompatible, but the reader's "fun" (as James called it) is in deciding whether or not they are. The game we must play as *Under Western Eyes* closes is still more complex, and the stakes are higher, since it is a matter of evaluating two great cultural spheres — Russia and "the West of Europe." Conrad's English narrator just stops *in medias res*, evidently unable to proceed, perhaps even unhinged.

Kermode's conclusion may be right, that in the end the novel "asserts the fallibility of all that it seems to assert." We may, if we like, infer that all the Russians except the Haldins and Tekla have been playing double games, or at least that the narrator is ready to think so. Certainly Razumov had to play such a game, and we learn from Sophia Antonovna that Mikulin and Peter Ivanovitch have been exchanging confidences in a railway carriage about Nikita, "who killed in both camps" (381). To account for such candor between the two camps, we must presume that either Peter Ivanovitch is a double agent or the Police Chief is, but the narrator leaves the issue unexamined.

We may go on to suspect that even Sophia Antonovna is beginning to play a double game. Her visits to Razumov back in Russia seem to portend agreement with him, that a true Russian must be "independent" of the revolution as well as the autocracy. ("He has ideas .... He talks well, too," she says of the now deafened derelict [379].) Hers are the novel's last words, spoken caustically one assumes: "Peter Ivanovitch is an inspired man" sarcastically echoes Tekla's doting tribute and her own former opinion of the contemptible man (237, 249-50). The English narrator (and many a reader, no doubt) gives up trying to fathom the depths of her ironies. As the narrator ends his book, simply parroting her enigmatic words, we scurry in search of some secure, hidden center of sanity.

Zabel's comment on this ending — in the first scholarly edition of *Under Western Eyes* (1951) — reflected a common American opinion in the post-war Stalinist era. The novel, he said, "leaves its question open . . . pending the moral decision of Europe and the West."[11] Zabel assumed that the novel could be read sympathetically only by "Europe and the West" — that it bears no devastating critique of "the West" such as (in my reading) would force some readers to prefer Razumov's "Eastern" point of view — in many respects — to the Western "eyes" offered us by the narrator. It may be that Conrad and Zabel both, if they had lived into the era of *glasnost* and *perestroika*, would still believe the Russians incapable of making the "moral decision" to end what the Author's Note called the "moral anarchism" of their "autocratic rule," inspiring the "atrocious answer of a purely Utopian revolutionism"(x). The novel's ending nevertheless probes the inadequacies of its Western stance to a point where some missing center — neither Eastern nor Western unless perhaps both — is required to save the novel itself from "moral anarchism." Kermode's 1974 essay puts it well, asserting that the novel's "last page . . . offers not closure but a hermeneutic booby-trap."[12] If the English narrator's commentary breeds suspicion, I have implied, a case could be made for trusting Razumov's judgment completely — as given both in the diary and in the narrator's reports.

III

One way of deciding the case would be to weigh the diarist's views against the English teacher's harshest criticism of them and see which reporter is finally the most persuasive. Such a reading would "work" in "The Secret Sharer" when deciding whether to believe Leggatt's report of the killing aboard the *Sephora* or the contradictory report of his captain, Archbold, for in that case there are only two witnesses to compare, and one of them is clearly lying. (What relief it must have given Conrad, while writing the

soul-wrenching, inconclusive *Under Western Eyes,* to bring
the analogous sea story to a hopeful and decisive conclusion, with the Haldin/Leggatt figure swimming free to a
"new destiny.") Conrad designed the Russian story with
many more "sides" to it, however. Most obviously, there
is in the sea story no such case against Leggatt as Razumov held against Haldin, a case that turns like a sword
in Razumov's hand when Haldin, under torture, refuses to
betray his betrayer and goes to his death protecting him.
In Geneva, Razumov's case against the revolutionaries who
have robbed him of his security is thus gradually eroded
not only by sympathy for Haldin but also by Razumov's
attraction to Natalia and growing disgust for the deceit he
must practice on her while serving as police spy. Much more
than in any of the Marlow tales, or indeed in any other mod-
ernist fiction, Conrad drives his story toward a conclusion
that can only be sorted out from among multiple choices
and multiple rejections. The Author's Note and the novel
itself heavily weigh in favor of some consensus that will be
fair to the Russians. This is no post-modernist novel such
as Frank Kermode envisions in its deliberate bafflements.[13]
But Conrad's determination to be just to all the players
prevented him from giving the game to any person or group
in the novel, either from Russia or "the West."

A sharper analogy for the novel's procedure would
aptly be drawn from the seaman's art. Something like the
navigator's true North is posited for the reader's finding.
Searching for it, one discovers that missing center of the
novel, needed to achieve the "prodigy of our knowing,"
which James considered Conrad's extraordinary quarry in
writing fiction. (He had also said to Conrad in 1906, "No
one has *known* — for intellectual use — the things you
know."[14] Conrad would appreciate James's distinction between what a mind can know and what it can know for

use.) The missing viewpoint of *Under Western Eyes* has to be found somewhat as with the sextant which the seaman Conrad used, sighting from the North Star to find a ship's position. The position of the reader at the end of the novel should be left in no more doubt than that if Conrad's claims for the novel's "general truth" are trustworthy.

The eye of the novel's narrator, assumed in its title and all the way through the novel, appears at first to be that "true North," forming the first angle (call it n) required for a sighting. Gradually, however, the reader (at angle R) comes to doubt that this n will indeed provide the ship's (*i.e.* the novel's) true position at S. To determine this, the reader must first discover that the narrator's triangulation (nRS1) gives a false reading. Once aware that the true reading is missing from the novel, one then looks beyond it — to N — an angle that completes one's reading by clarifying the triangle RNS2 (see diagram). To find a footing that is both secure and fitting to all the novel tells us of *cosas de Russia*, we have to sight by something that is "light years away" from both the narrator and ourselves.

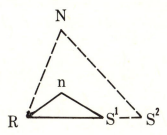

R = reader
n = narrator
N = missing center ("North Star")
S^1 = Razumov's story as narrator tells it
S^2 = Razumov's story as corrected from missing center

This steady, strange, and distant point is best described as a viewpoint that is Slavic but not Russian or Polish, and also European but not English. The viewpoint has, in fact, no *nationality* but takes its character from the best we can derive from the novel's testimonies in support of the Russians on one side and the Westerner, or non-Russian, on the other. Some ideal is posited by the novel, in other words, that reconciles two types of humanity, stripped of their worst traits. This ideal combines a Slavic passion for self-assertion and liberation ("as a hungry man would snatch a piece of bread," the epigraph says) with a Western respect for political reason and self-control. Conrad was himself in process of integrating two such mentalities when he wrote *Under Western Eyes,* and this may account for some of the curious features of the manuscript discussed by David Smith and Keith Carabine in the present collection. Remembering Conrad's changes of mind as to his own Slavic and Western attitudes may help us further in explaining why he doodled his own initials so often in the manuscript and confusedly intruded his own opinions initially into the minds of both Razumov and his prosecutor, the English teacher.

Everyone must be aware by now that Conrad wholeheartedly supported Panslavonism and considered himself a Slav before he took British citizenship in 1886. As proof, we have commonly cited his uncle Tadeusz Bobrowski's letter of September 23, 1881, trying to convince the twenty-three year old Conrad that Panslavonism could serve only Russian ambitions in the world. At that point Conrad was himself opposed to "westerners" — Slavs unlike himself at the time who were Anglophiles and Francophiles (Hay, 18). No one has noticed, I believe, that Conrad continued to call himself a Slav long after his British naturalization and began insisting that he was "Western" much later than we supposed, some while after finishing *Under Western Eyes*. I fear that I helped to obscure the fact ((ibid., 2, 300). When Razumov bitterly hears himself called "a regular Englishman" by Haldin (22), we should remember Conrad's self-portrait of himself, painted later in *The Arrow of Gold*, as a young Slav in France who is renamed M. George (surname of Conrad's English wife, the use of it a family joke one suspects).

I have become unsure indeed when Conrad did stop calling himself a Slav. Certainly he was still bothered by the Slavic "westerners" in 1899 when he wrote to Cunninghame Graham that he would avoid any meeting where they were present (*CL*, II:158). And he was still calling himself a Slav in October, 1907, when he raged to Garnett about his review of *The Secret Agent*: "You remember always that I am a Slav (it's your idée fixe), but you seem to forget that I am a Pole," he wrote (*LG*, 209). In the same letter he distanced himself, as he often did, from the English, telling Garnett that "you Britishers . . . 'go in to win' only," meaning that the English are incapable of fighting from conviction alone, like the Slav (Polish) hero of Conrad's "Prince Roman" (1912). This implied that the English were motivated only by material rewards, which appears to be the case with the English narrator of *Under Western Eyes*, despite his protests against his niece in the manuscript. Anyway it is hard to imagine otherwise why he "goes in" for teaching languages or writes his book if he denies the non-material value of his profession, words ("the foes of reality").

Just before beginning *Under Western Eyes*, Conrad wrote to Galsworthy again defining himself as a Slav and writing against the English. Referring apprehensively to Garnett's attitude, he told Galsworthy, "as a Slav, I know nothing of the English temper in controversy" (*CL*, III:503). This confession of ignorance helps explain why the novel's

English narrator is such a cipher and why the manuscript presents him at varying distances from Razumov's point of view as well as from the "missing center" of the novel.

Evidently it was the First World War that made Conrad for the first time assert his own and Poland's "Western" mentality. After 1914, when he revisited Poland for the first time since 1893, he began to see the chance for a free Poland to separate itself from the Slavic world and join itself politically to "the West of Europe," as the English teacher calls "us," his privileged readers. In 1916 Conrad published his "Note on the Polish Problem," contradicting not only the stand taken in his twenties but the one he held while writing *Under Western Eyes*. Thus it was only nine years later that he claimed for the first time to have "Western" eyes himself:

> The Poles, whom superficial or ill-informed theorists are trying to force into the social and psychological formula of Slavonism, are in truth not Slavonic at all. In temperament, in feeling, in mind, and even in unreason, they are Western, with an absolute comprehension of all Western modes of thought, even those which are remote from their historical experience [e.g., the Puritan — as indicated in such characters as Podmore and Holroyd] (*NLL*, 135).[15]

The phrase "even in unreason" points to the Romantic side of English character that Martin Decoud in *Nostromo* had called Charles Gould's liking for fairy tales (as in his idealized conception of the silver mine). But this English taste for unreason that is shared by the Poles was notably lacking in the English narrator of *Under Western Eyes*. It was rather his resistance to the political idealism of Razumov and the Haldins that he prided himself on. His cool pragmatism could always be considered an English trait, but in the passage just cited Conrad may well include English pragmatism as a "mode" of Western thought "remote from [Poland's] historical experience."

It is fair to conclude, then, on both intertextual and intratextual grounds, that *Under Western Eyes* presupposes a central point of view that is foreign to the English narrator and is indeed nowhere represented in the novel. By design, this missing center is neither "Eastern" nor "Western" and is not even Polish or a possession of the implied author. Concerned as Conrad was to be just, he gave the lion's share of *feeling* to three very attractive Russians, and their feelings are all the more poignant because they are forced by circumstances to cynicism, treason, and brutality. The English narrator legitimately holds the lion's share of *reason*, but his mode of thinking so nearly denatures his account that Conrad needed to defend his narrative as deliberately "a performance on one string" (*LG*, 234). We remember that he feared the alternative would be a Dostoevskian "debauch of the imagination" — if either Razumov or some narrator closer to Conrad' s own point of view had provided the principal intelligence in the novel. Being English and a stiff suspecter of words, the narrator Conrad chose created a tactical gap, even a void, between himself and the good Russians in the novel (the others being "fair game" Conrad said in the Author's Note [ix]) — a gap between two irreconcilable points of view. Since neither is finally acceptable in resolving the issues raised concerning revolution and autocracy, "passionless" democracy and a better political alternative, readers are left to find a satisfactory position of their own.

This third standpoint, or missing center, at which careful readers will arrive if they use the sextant that Conrad himself supplies, is made necessary and certain in two main ways: first by our perception of strengths and deficiencies in the characters that are evident but unidentified by the narrator (e.g. Razumov's acute sense of truth and his own callousness in responding to Natalia's pain); second by our awareness of novels Conrad had earlier published that serve as guideposts peripherally to truths he constantly asserted. Several constituents of the missing point of view emerge from such clues.

First would be that sympathetic imagination which the English teacher so strangely lacks. Conrad's son John remembered that his father often stressed the need "to come alongside of people" — a shipping term for the gift of understanding that distinguishes Jim's Marlow and Leggatt's secret sharer, in fact all of Conrad's narrators unless they are deliberately deprived of this gift.[16] A second essential to the central point of view that is missing in *Under Western Eyes* would be conscious attention to the importance of work. Although the English narrator conveys Razumov's anguish over finding — and losing — the work he is preparing for, his awareness is a reflection of Razumov's own concern in the diary and seems not to relate at all to any work ethic of the narrator's. Third, the novel's narrator has no such concern for the future of his homeland as the "good Russians" intensely demonstrate for theirs, the concern that in other novels Marlow so eloquently expresses, as does the narrator of *The Nigger of the "Narcissus"* and as the implied author does in *Nostromo* and *The Rover*, to mention prominent cases. Because the English teacher has little concern about belonging in his homeland, we glean our compassion for the Russians' forced emigration in spite rather than because of him and respect Razumov and Natalia for their return to Russia in the end more than we respect the cosmopolitan Englishman for his continuing residence in the Geneva he so dislikes.

Another, fourth, central value that the reader supplies from awareness of its absence in the narrator's judgments is the need all the other "good" characters express for some community rule or order. In Conrad's sea fiction, the desired order is supplied by ships. On land the order may be supplied by a domestic woman (Emilia Gould or Winnie Verloc) or may be defined politically by visionaries like Dr. Monygham or Natalia Haldin. The order longed for by Razumov, Haldin, and his sister in their different ways is of course not actualized, but it is made an urgent matter through their dedication and through its travesty by the Russian autocracy. Furthermore, the English narrator's very thrusts against it incline one to believe in this powerful dream, especially when it is weighed against the actual but frigid democracy represented in the city of his choice.

Finally, missing from his narrative is any truly transnational, or supra-national, point of view — such a view as exists very powerfully in *Lord Jim* and all of Conrad's other major fiction. Much as Conrad himself (like Razumov) recoiled from the internationalism of revolutionaries, he had a strong sense of "fellowship with all creation"[17] — across national boundaries — that appears strangely missing in the claustral Russian groups and in the "eyes" — the only non-Russian eyes — of this novel.

So the "Western eyes" of the title, insofar as they have a clear reference point at all, conceal the very eyes we may need to read the novel with. America is left out of the picture for reasons we considered in Conrad's deletions from the manuscript. As far as Europe is concerned, what Conrad said in "Autocracy and War" (1905) applies forcefully to *Under Western Eyes*: *"Il n'y a plus d'Europe* — there is only an armed and trading continent, the home of slowly maturing economical contests for life and death, and of loudly proclaimed world-wide ambitions" (*NLL*, 112). "[T]he architectural aspect of the universal city remains as yet inconceivable — [and] the very ground for its erection has not been cleared of the jungle" (107). The jungle metaphor reappears in the Note for *Under Western Eyes* where Conrad defends his characterization of the pernicious Russians, calling them "fair game" in a "sinister jungle." *Under Western Eyes* is unique among Conrad's novels, however, for providing no one in the novel who can even begin to clear the jungle — no one except the novel's readers, whose sympathies and antipathies must move them to decide whether or not a just society can be built in Russia.

Perhaps Conrad deliberately rigged the novel's ending to have us conclude that the Russian "tiger cannot change his stripes nor the leopard his spots," his last words in the Author's Note. But this was written right after the Bolshevik Revolution and does not really cancel the more hopeful stand he took earlier in 1905, in "Autocracy and War," after the defeat of Russia by Japan in that year. There, sounding as optimistic as Natalia Haldin and almost in identical words, he anticipated in the distant future "the advent of Concord and Justice . . . the only possible goal of our progress" (97). The same passage links achievement of this goal to "the solidarity of Europeanism," seeming to confirm Zabel's reading of the novel's ending as an appeal to "Europe and the West" rather than to any change of hearts in Russia. Still, I must observe again that — even in "Autocracy and War" — Conrad found no evidence of European solidarity. Nor had he any trust in the wisdom of "the West" while writing *Under Western Eyes*, not until the First World War provided some evidence of unified action in the West and created an intellectual climate for more. To the contrary, in 1905 (as seven years earlier in the last paragraphs of "Youth") it was "the East" that possessed the greater strength:

> The West having managed to lodge its hasty foot on the neck of the East is prone to forget that it is from the East

that the wonders of patience and wisdom have come to a world of men who set the value of life in the power to act rather than in the faculty of meditation.

Action, in which is to be found the illusion of a mastered destiny, can alone satisfy our uneasy vanity and lay to rest the haunting fear of the future .... And the only form of action open to a State can be of no other than aggressive nature ("Autocracy and War," *NLL*, 88, 109).

If "Western" eyes are not to be altogether trusted, then, and we concede that the ending of the novel sets a booby-trap, the reader may agree to the charge of nihilism brought lately by hasty readers of Conrad's work. But this would be to accuse him of the very "negation of everything worth living for," leaving the "yawning chasm between East and West," that he charged to the account of Russia itself in "Autocracy and War" (100).

Alternatively, one can respond to the "good Russian" whom Conrad consistently recognized amid his worst indictments of Russia (*NLL*, 93, *APR*, 65–66) and typified in *Under Western Eyes* — in the Haldins, in Tekla, and above all in Razumov. They alone in the novel possess that virtue *sine qua non*: that "sympathetic imagination, to which alone we can look for the ultimate triumph of concord and justice" (*NLL*, 84). The lack of this quality, when the novel's narrator conspicuously fails to "come alongside" his chief subject, Razumov, in the last two-thirds of the novel, impels the reader to seek, find, or even create that missing center where we should be creative and also particularly wary of "Western eyes."

NOTES

[1] Henry James, "The New Novel," *Literary Criticism: Essays on Literature, American Writers, English Writers* (New York: The Library of America, 1984), p. 148.

[2] Ernest Dowson, *The Letters of Ernest Dowson*, ed. Desmond Flower and Henry Maas (Rutherford, NJ: Fairleigh Dickinson U.P., 1967), p. 146.

[3] "The New Novel," pp. 148–9.

[4] Although Morton Dauwen Zabel confirms Conrad's assertions and says that *Under Western Eyes* was serialized both in Moscow and St. Petersburg in the popular magazine *Wiestnik Europy*, others have doubted Conrad's claim, saying that only a small "edition" of 1,200 copies appeared in Russia during his lifetime. See Zabel's Introduction to *Under Western Eyes* (New York: New Directions, 1951 [rev. 1963]), xiii–xiv; but against Conrad see Eugene Steele in *Conradiana* 14:1 (1982) and Roderick Davis in *L'Epoque conradienne* (Limoges, 1988).

[5] In the course of discussions at the California Institute of Technology.

[6] Frank Kermode, "Novel and Narrative," *The Theory of the Novel*, ed. John Halperin (New York: Oxford U.P., 1974), p. 173.

[7] Albert Guerard, *Conrad the Novelist* (Cambridge, MA: Harvard U.P., 1958), p. 245.

[8] "Note on the Polish Problem," *NLL*, pp. 135, 137.

[9] Friederich Schlegel, *Athenaeum* Fragment 125, *Kritische Ausgabe*, ed. Ernst Behler. 35 vols. (München: Ferdinand Schöningh, 1958–80), II. Translation mine.

[10] David Leon Higdon, "Conrad, *Under Western Eyes*, and the Mysteries of Revision," *Review of English Studies*, 39:54, p. 237.

[11] Zabel, "Introduction," p. xxxvi.

[12] Kermode, "Novel and Narrative," p. 173.

[13] Frank Kermode, "Secrets and Narrative Sequence," *Essays on Fiction, 1971–82* (London: Routledge and Kegan Paul, 1983), pp. 133–155. In this 1980 essay, Kermode says that *Un-*

der Western Eyes is "disingenuous from the preface on . . . in a sense it hates its readers." This follows from his interpretation of the English narrator as "the father of lies," "a diabolical narrator." Here Kermode impressively confronts the "secrets," "ghosts," and "phantoms" in the language of the novel, but we need to consider that these gothic elements (derived perhaps from Conrad's Polish medievalisms) are at least as plentiful in the language of *Lord Jim* and therefore not specific to *Under Western Eyes.*

[14] Henry James, *Letters: Volume IV, 1895–1916*, ed. Leon Edel (Cambridge: Belknap Press, 1984), p. 419.

[15] *Notes on Life and Letters*, p. 135. See also his letter of Dec. 14, 1922, to Keating in *LL*, II:289. "Slavonism . . . . cannot possibly apply to me. Racially I belong to a group . . . with a Western Roman culture derived from France . . . . [The Russian mentality shown in Russian novels] and their emotionalism have always been repugnant to me . . . . I am a child, not of a savage but of a chivalrous tradition, and if my mind took a tinge from anything it was from French romanticism perhaps." Remarkably here, while Conrad rejects the label of "Slav" which he had accepted from Garnett as late as 1907, he repossesses the Roman (or Latin) legacy that Marlow (English of course) made repugnant in *Heart of Darkness*. Not long before the letter to Keating, in writing the "Author's Note" for *Lord Jim*, Conrad defended Jim's "Latin" sense of honor. It would appear that he was consistent at least in defending the Roman origins of his heritage, whether early (when he considered it Slavic) or late (when he called it Western).

[16] This remark made in an interview I had with John Conrad in May, 1956, appears also (less emphatically) in his *Conrad: Times Remembered* (Cambridge: Cambridge U.P., 1981), p. 57.

[17] *The Nigger of the "Narcissus,"* p. viii.

Crossing the Dark Roadway: Razumov on the Boulevard des Philosophes

Roderick Davis

When Olive Garnett wrote to Conrad upon the publication of *Under Western Eyes*, praising the novel as "true," Conrad's reply discounted the verisimilitude of the Russian elements in the work as relatively unimportant. He wrote back: "In the book, as you must have seen, I am exclusively concerned with ideas."[1] Developing this theme in a letter with a more defensive tone written to her brother Edward on the same day, he exclaimed: "Is it possible that you haven't seen that in this book I am concerned with nothing but ideas, to the exclusion of everything else, with no arrière pensée of any kind."[2]

With that end in view, the author appropriately introduces Razumov, the novel's central figure, as a student at St. Petersburg University. However, for someone as bent as Razumov is on winning the prize that would give him "a claim to an administrative appointment of the better sort after he had taken his degree"(*UWE*, 8) — especially writing a prize essay on "The Government Reforms of Peter the Great"[3] — he is, surprisingly, not engaged in the study of law. Instead, he is described as a third-year student of

155

philosophy. While such an identification may serve to signal to a reader the philosophical focus that Conrad intends the book to have, there seems to be more than just general significance in Razumov's course of study.

Before considering his philosophical studies, it must be remembered that they occur in the milieu of Tsarist, mystical, oppressive Mother Russia. Conrad wrote about Razumov in the "Author's Note" that "Being nobody's child he feels rather more keenly than another would that he is a Russian — or he is nothing" (ix). He has the most Russian of names, Kirylo Sidorovitch Razumov. His Christian name and patronymic recall the saints Cyril and Isidore, suggesting his supposed heritage as the grandson of an archpriest and, through Cyril, his quintessential Russianness, in paying homage to the famous "Apostle to the Slavs" who invented the Glagolithic alphabet, which is now named after him, and thus founded Slavonic literature.

This rootage in the Church is joined with a surname. "Razumov," though, is not the name of his real father. However he got it, that name suggests his position as a rational person within the irrational immensity that is Russia. Its meaning could refer also to more than reason in a general sense. In Russian philosophy of the mid-nineteenth century *razum* was a philosophic term with a more specific reference. It was A. S. Khomyakor who defined and employed the term *razum* (=Vernunft) integral reason, which is opposed to *rassudok* (=Verstand), fragmented understanding. Khomyakor was known for opposing the "pure rationalism" and "pure materialism" of Hegel and Feuerbach as deterministic, as denying freedom and subjectivity. Khomyakor held that the exercise of *razum* — or reason in faith — brings men together in a communal consciousness.[4] This, however, is not an exercise Conrad's solitary Razumov is known for employing. He has neither faith nor friends and family. But we do not name ourselves at birth, and his name might be an ironic comment on how far removed he is from what his archpriest grandfather hoped from him and from Russia — and from God.

Philosophy students in Russian universities, until this century, studied under professors who were rarely independent thinkers on a par with their counterparts in western Europe and tended more or less to function as disciples of some Western master. For that reason, as Peter Kropotkin wrote in 1905:

> In no other country does literature occupy so influential a position as it does in Russia. Nowhere else does it exercise so profound and so direct an influence upon the intellectual development of the younger generation .... The reason why . . . is self-evident. There is no open political life .... The consequence has been that the best minds of the country have chosen the poem, the novel, the satire, or literary criticism as the medium for expressing their aspirations, their conceptions of national life, or their ideals.[5]

Philosophy students read also what we would call critics, as well as authors like Dostoevsky and Tolstoy, Gogol, A.A. Blok, and Andrei Bely, who are among the many writers who have been more than usually interested in recurrent philosophical and quasi-philosophical problems, and who often suffered at the hands of the state for their pains.

Further, because many philosophers in Russia tended to write with a special intensity and an impatience with moderation, they were virtually excluded from academic life. As a reaction to the Decembrist uprising of 1825, instruction in philosophy was forbidden in Russian universities until 1863. Even after that, all that was officially permitted until as late as 1889 were lecture-commentaries on selected Platonic and Aristotelian texts.[6]

There would seem to be a reference in the novel to philosophy's academically restricted past condition when

Razumov meets Councillor Mikulin. This official is later
seen as "a clever but faithful official . . . with reforming
tendencies" — an older version of Razumov himself, perhaps, at the very least his secret sharer — "the only person on earth with whom Razumov could talk" (304). Earlier,
the older man tries to establish some common ground with
the student, asserting that "When I was young like you I
studied . . . " (97), but Razumov breaks him off before he
can finish, apparently afraid of learning that this neme-
sis was once so like himself. Nevertheless, throughout the
novel there are suggestions that Mikulin might well have
been a student of Greek philosophy a generation earlier. He
is constantly associated with things Hellenic. He has Epi-
curean tastes, discusses Razumov's case with Prince K—
"like two Olympians," (306) and endures his own fall with
bureaucratic Stoicism. He lectures Razumov on what the
ancient Greeks understood (294) and is described as wearing
a signet ring set with "a blood-red stone" that looked "as if
it could weigh half a pound . . . an appropriate ornament
for that ponderous man with . . . a rugged Socratic fore-
head" (90). This perhaps is meant to suggest that Councillor
Mikulin, not having succeeded at finding the philosopher's
stone, has now settled for the Inquisitor's — one that is far
less rare, but one undoubtedly of more material worth.

In response to his interrogation by Mikulin, Razumov
alludes to Pascal's *Pensées* in making his defense: "I know I
am but a reed. But I beg you to allow me the superiority of
the thinking reed over the unthinking forces that are about
to crush him out of existence."[7]

He is chided by Mikulin: " 'You are angry,' remarked
the official, with an unutterable simplicity of tone and manner. 'Is that reasonable?' " Razumov replies:

"I am reasonable. I am even — permit me to say — a
thinker, though to be sure, this name nowadays seems to

be the monopoly of hawkers of revolutionary wares, the slaves of some French or German thought — devil knows what foreign notions. But I am not an intellectual mongrel. I think like a Russian. I think faithfully — and I take the liberty to call myself a thinker. It is not a forbidden word, as far as I know . . . . "

"Why should it be forbidden? . . . I too consider myself a thinking man, I assure you. The principal condition is to think correctly. I admit it is difficult sometimes at first for a young man abandoned to himself — with his generous impulses undisciplined, so to speak — at the mercy of every wild wind that blows. Religious belief, of course is a great . . . . "

Councillor Mikulin glanced down his beard, and Razumov, whose tension was relaxed by that unexpected and discursive turn murmured with gloomy discontent — "That man, Haldin, believed in God."

"Ah! You are aware," breathed out Councillor Mikulin, making the point softly, as if with discretion, but making it nevertheless plainly enough . . . (89–91).

Razumov may be a thinker, but this passage demonstrates that he is not one who is quick enough to avoid being trapped by Mikulin — much as Dostoevsky's Raskolnikov was boxed in by Porfiry.

Razumov's attempt in that dialogue to establish his patriotic loyalties by making denigrating references to French and German thinkers recalls that such foreign philosophers were officially proscribed in Russia. However, from about 1830 on, informal discussion groups — *kruzhki,* "circles," — commonly met outside the universities to read and heatedly discuss forbidden German metaphysics and French social theory, often in samizdat translations.[8] For Razumov to have studied philosophy, he would have had to undergo some risk in this regard. The allusion to his having met Haldin "from time to time at other students' houses"(15) suggests perhaps that Razumov was not entirely the timid careerist that is elsewhere indicated.

At any rate, to study philosophy in Russia was not quite the same as in the West, where it would be more likely to be pursued as a "pure" discipline, whereas Russian intellectuals viewed ideas more instrumentally, as weapons to break down barriers to freedom. The Russians would have viewed the study of pure philosophy as an evasion of urgent moral and sociopolitical problems. To the Russian intelligentsia, theoretical truth (*istina*) was subordinate to practical truth and justice (*pravda*).[9] In *Under Western Eyes*, the terrorist Victor Haldin is representative of this view, if in an extreme way.

But Razumov is less easily categorized. In the manuscript of the novel, there is an interesting omission in the early scene where, as Haldin reveals to Razumov that he has removed Minister of State de P—, the assassin exclaims, "But God of Justice! This is weary work." And "Razumov, in his chair, leaning his head on his hand, spoke as if from the bottom of an abyss. 'You believe in God, Haldin?'" Haldin answers: "There you go catching at words that are wrung from one"(23). But the manuscript has Haldin replying: "There you go with your western skepticism catching at words that are wrung from one" (MS 67).

The omission of this phrase from the final text suggests that Conrad realized ultimately that he did not quite want to identify his Russian student so openly or completely as a product of Western thought or of a particularly Western philosophical attitude, however credible it might be, given the appeal it had. Nevertheless, removing that Western attribution does not remove the philosophy from Razumov himself, as can be seen in Haldin's assertion to him, sounding like a precursor of Aleksandr Solzhenitsyn, that

> The modern civilization is false, but a new revelation shall come out of Russia. Ha! you say nothing. You are a skeptic. I respect your philosophical skepticism, Razumov, but

don't touch the soul. The Russian soul that lives in all of us. It has a future. It has a mission, I tell you, or why else should I have been moved to do this . . . (22).

There is also an indication of Razumov's metaphysical skepticism in his statement at the end of the agonized scene where he — whom Natalia Haldin does not yet know to be the betrayer of her brother — has just broken the news to her that Victor has now been executed. Observing the sister's awful suffering as a result of this disclosure, his immediate reaction, his desperate reach for some solace for himself takes this form: " 'It's lucky I don't believe in another world,' he had thought cynically"(339).

That delineation of Razumov's metaphysical position remained in the published novel, although other similar items in the manuscript were omitted. One such omission is in the novel's opening section where the teacher of languages speaks of Razumov's diary:

> In places he apostrophises the Deity with considerable violence and bitterness. But this violence and bitterness are robbed of all offensively blasphemous quality by the consideration that Mr. Razumov held no religious faith or belief of any kind (MS 3).

Skepticism, as a critical philosophical position with a vital history in Western civilization, was defined by Timon in the 3rd century B.C. as "a practical, moral way of living according to human necessities without making any grandiose commitments or claims." His follower Sextus Empiricus saw it as something like Keat's negative capability, developing arguments while employing suspension of judgment about matters dealing with what is nonevident.[10]

Pierre Bayle, "perhaps the most incisive of the modern skeptics . . . sought to show that most theories 'are big with contradiction and absurdity' and that man's efforts to comprehend the world in rational terms always end in perplexities, bewilderment, and insoluble difficulties," writes Richard Popkin.[11] Bayle's critique of traditional religion was influential with many European skeptics, and Voltaire, Diderot, and others followed his lead.

Among the most significant skeptics was René Descartes, whose doubts were so thorough that he rejected all beliefs rendered dubious by the skeptical problems about sense experience, by the possibility that all that we know is part of a dream (a theory that appeared also in Montaigne), and by the possibility that there may be a demon who distorts our judgment — (a new skeptical possibility which he introduced).[12] There are elements of Descartes' thought in Razumov's recurring sense of his life as a dream, one haunted by apparitions and demons.

Pascal speaks of dreams, too, in *Pensé* 386, as their effect on us being less than that of our waking life because "it changes less abruptly, except rarely, as when we travel, and then we say, 'It seems to me I am dreaming.' For life is a dream a little less inconstant." Compare Razumov's journey from Russia:

> then the dream had him again: Prussia, Saxony, Würtemberg, faces, sights, words — all a dream, observed with an angry, compelled attention. Zürich, Geneva — still a dream, minutely followed, wearing one into harsh laughter, to fury, to death — with the fear of awakening at the end . . . (315–316).

Pascal also stated the case for ultimate and complete skepticism about as strongly as it has ever been done. But he contended that, no matter how much reason leads us to doubt, "I lay it down as a fact that there never has been a real complete skeptic. Nature sustains our feeble reason, and prevents it raving to this extent."[13]

It is conceivable that Razumov, stripped of all the supports of a family, a profession, a country, and a future, starting out with no metaphysical beliefs and having his remaining political and social ones knocked out from under him, was envisioned by Conrad as an argument against that claim of Pascal's. For example, Razumov could look on Mrs. Haldin after he had broken the news to her of Victor's death, and could shrug off his brief "pitying surprise" at her grief with the assertion to himself that "Mothers did not matter"(287). In the manuscript, a stronger echo of Nietzsche and Raskolnikov was deleted which said, "That old woman was of no importance"(MS 1258). Setting aside the appealing innocence of Natalia Haldin, there is absolutely nothing that Razumov finds to believe in, certainly not family or country — and least of all in the end, in himself.

After sending the unsuspecting Haldin out into the trap that will doom him, Razumov attempts to justify his action, at least to himself, through setting down on paper a sort of credo made up of a series of political-philosophical catch phrases that are common in the literature of European and Russian philosophical schools of previous generations as well as his own. He writes:

> History not Theory
> Patriotism not Internationalism
> Evolution not Revolution
> Direction not Destruction
> Unity not Disruption (66)

This accumulation of reactionary slogans shows a desperate grasping for something to hold on to. It is possible to read these phrases as generally referring to particular philosophers: "Direction not Destruction" rejects most obviously Michael Bakunin's revolutionary philosophy, and "Evolution not Revolution" is perhaps an endorsement of the Russian biologist Karl von Baer's idealistic theory of purposeful evolution, which also influenced Peter

Kropotkin and N.K. Mikhailovsky. But the first of these pronouncements, "History not Theory," surely refers to the ideas of G.W.F. Hegel, who had enormous influence on Russian philosophy in the nineteenth century. Hegel's basic conviction that history makes sense has pervaded Russian thought down to the present, creating an appeal that Russian Communism has tried to appropriate for its own uses. Hegel's famous assertion that "the real is rational and the rational is real" gave young Russians of his time and afterwards the belief that the only salvation from madness — even that of life under Tsar Nicholas I — is history.[14]

Razumov declares this belief in history as his first principle, also. But when he reflects on it in perhaps the most harrowing passage in the novel, he despairs:

> He stared in dreary astonishment at the absurdity of his position. He thought with a sort of dry, unemotional melancholy; three years of good work gone, the course of forty more perhaps jeopardized — turned from hope to terror, because events started by human folly link themselves into a sequence which no sagacity can foresee and no courage can break through. Fatality enters your rooms while your landlady's back is turned; you come home and find it in possession bearing a man's name, clothed in flesh — wearing a brown cloth coat and long boots — lounging against the stove. It asks you, "Is the outer door closed?" — and you don't know enough to take it by the throat and fling it downstairs. You don't know. You welcome the crazy fate. "Sit down," you say. And it is all over. You cannot shake it off any more. It will cling to you for ever. Neither halter nor bullet can give you back the freedom of your life and the sanity of your thought .... It was enough to make one dash one's head against a wall (83–84).

This paragraph poses the philosophical issue that pervades the entire novel. It is this question that lies at the heart of Razumov's story. How is even such an exemplar of the life of rationality as young Razumov, as dedicated as a monk to the study of philosophy itself, to live a rational and ordered life in a world in which, when we may least expect it, we are always vulnerable to the destructive caprices of irrationality's violence and anarchy, which in a moment's notice can ruin our lives?

The ultimate result of all his absorption of so much of Western philosophy — which shaped him as all Europe contributed to the making of Mr. Kurtz — is how inadequately it has prepared Razumov to respond wisely in a time of crisis to the test of what he calls "crazy fate" requires of him. He, who would above all in his mind be free, shows himself to be a slave of his ego, then a cat's-paw of the state. He fails himself as badly as does that other philosophy student in St. Petersburg, Dostoevsky's Raskolnikov, or that one-time student at the university in Conrad's home town of Cracow, Dr. Johann Faust.

Consequently, after his betrayal of Haldin to Councillor Mikulin results in his being forced to see how little faith he also can now have in the state, Prince K—, or his own future in Russia, the situation he finds himself in as he attempts "to retire" becomes all the more poignant when he has to face the question asked by Mikulin: "Where to?"

It is therefore important for the contrast that, shorn of all his previous supports, it should be to Geneva that Razumov is transported. It is to the city that has given refuge to Huguenots and heretics, philosophers and *agents provocateurs*. What city in Europe could be more a contrast to St. Petersburg and the horror of trying to live an ordered and intellectually free life under a despotic and whimsically cruel tyrant than Geneva, with its placid democratic rule that allowed the freedom and individuality that Russia so fiercely denied? Where were there greater differences than between St. Petersburg's Dostoevsky, with his searing probing of human depravity, with redemption through suffering and the mystical ties of man to man, motherland, and the Orthodox God, on the one hand and, on the other, Geneva's *Philosophes?* These men in varying degrees were all committed to a materialistic philosophy, essentially determinism, but at the same time trying to maintain an emotional faith in progress, civilization, and the social virtues of kindess, unselfishness, and public-spiritedness — despite the illogicality of there being any moral responsibility if our lives are predetermined by physical and chemical laws.

Conrad could expect that Razumov would be familiar with Voltaire, Rousseau, and the Encyclopedists. Ever since Diderot's visit to the Petersburg court of Catherine the Great in 1773-74, the attitudes and doctrines of the *Philosophes*, especially skepticism and rationalism (in the sense of hostility toward tradition, superstition, and obscurantism) were well known among Russian intellectuals.[15]

Razumov perhaps knew, for example, Diderot's *Rameau's Nephew*, a work which, among other things, is a discussion of dilemmas that confront moral man in an immoral society. The two protagonists' long discussion of the relative merits of being a genius or being a good man seem to be echoed in Razumov's scornful comment to himself that "I had neither the simplicity nor the courage nor the self-possession to be a scoundrel, or an exceptionally able man. For who, with us in Russia, is to tell a scoundrel from an exceptionally able man?" (362)

Diderot was never able to resolve in his writings the contradiction in being, as Leonard Tancock puts it: "illogically both a materialistic fatalist and a sentimental moralist."[16] Like so many other eighteenth-century thinkers, he tried to maintain both the materialistic view of life that is really determinism along with an emotional faith in the private and social virtues, civilization, and progress. His contention that doubt was the beginning of wisdom and often its end would perhaps find its objective correlative in Conrad's various descriptions of the Boulevard des Philosophes as a "singularly arid and dusty thoroughfare," as "empty," and as "hopeless" to both the suffering Mrs. Haldin, who looks out on it daily, and Razumov, who haplessly crosses its "dark roadway" in search of some meaning in or resolution to his own torment.

Rousseau, who of course broke with the *Philosophes* as he did with Voltaire, Hume, the city fathers of Geneva, and virtually every one else — preferring to be largely removed from humanity while writing his *Social Contract* and other works on how mankind should live — is another solitary and fellow exile. The bronze effigy of this philosopher who expounded man's innate goodness and democracy's excellence as a system of government — but only for people who are so mature that they can govern themselves anyway — this statue sits "enthroned" on the tiny, pretentious, shabby Ile Rousseau with poised pen looming over the bowed head of Razumov as he writes his secret report for the Tsarist police. The influence of the Geneva philosopher may be partly responsible for this composition being full of its author's conceit and disdain for his fellows. The report is perhaps in the ignoble tradition that Conrad refers to in *A Personal Record*, "confessions" that are "a form of literary activity discredited by Jean Jacques Rousseau on account of the extreme thoroughness he brought to the work of justifying his own existence" (95).

His intense dislike of Rousseau and what he understood to be his views can be seen in a number of Conrad's works, particularly because of the anarchy that those views threatened. It is obviously about Rousseau that Conrad speaks at the end of the "Author's Note" to *Under Western Eyes* when he mentions "the strange conviction that a fundamental change of hearts must follow the downfall of any given human institutions. These people are unable to see that all they can effect is merely a change of names"(38). Furthermore, Conrad's devotion to duty, fidelity, honor, constraint, and loyalty to one's fellows find no place in Rousseau's systems. And a belief in inner discipline puts him at odds with Rousseau's unreconciled views that discipline is both unnecessary and should be imposed from without. That contradiction in Rousseau's thought is seen also among the revolutionaries in Geneva, as the Teklas are oppressed still while the Peter Ivanovitches and Madame de S——es indulge themselves in gâteaux. But with Rousseau, as Zdzisław Najder has pointed out:

> we are . . . dealing with an opposition-obsession syndrome: although Conrad's reaction to Rousseau was predominantly negative, the ideas he condemned left on him an indelible imprint.[17]

Actually, there was much that the two had in common. Both men were educated largely on their own and became members of the intelligentsia, lived off their writings, moved about a lot in societies they were critical of but toward which they felt political and intellectual responsibilities, and, of course, both were exiles without strong communal bonds, though Conrad manifested a solidarity with the broader human community that Rousseau could not manage.

But Conrad sees democracy as Rousseau set it forth as the tyranny of the majority that de Toqueville feared, or else the banal life of Geneva's *juste-milieu* lived by the uncouth and vapid Swiss couple whose faces are as blank as that other void in the novel: the Russian immensity, with its *meshchanstvo*, bourgeois philistinism, and *posredstvennost*, mediocrity. If this is what the general will of the people results in, Conrad would perhaps agree with Harry Lime, in the screenplay of Graham Greene's "The Third Man," when he says:

In Italy for 30 years, under the Borgias, they had war-fare, terror, murder, and bloodshed, but they produced Michelangelo, Leonardo da Vinci, and the Renaissance. In Switzerland they had brotherly love. They had 500 years of democracy and peace, and what did that produce? The cuckoo clock!"

There is also one other *Philosophe* who is mentioned by name in the novel, Voltaire (105). G. Jean-Aubry tells us that Conrad had "une grande sympathie pour [l'esprit] de Voltaire et son oeuvre,"[18] and that affection would seem to be indicated by some very general similarities between this novel and Voltaire's most famous work. Razumov is not a Candide, but they are both rather naïve young men forced to travel from their homelands and the turmoil there, Candide in the thrall of Dr. Pangloss's optimistic determinism and Razumov under the thumb of both Councillor Mikulin and his own patchwork philosophy of reactionary abstractions. Both are also looking for the best in *this* world rather than the next. Both encounter a variety of human monsters manipulating others for their own ends under philosophic rationales of considerable cynicism. And the emotions of both are engaged by an innocent young woman from their own country who is also exiled and forced to suffer terribly by the novel's end.

Both *Candide* and *Under Western Eyes* are novels of ideas that propose to study the quirks of fate and the disordered complexity of existence as it affects their characters' lives. Each takes the protagonist to a comparative paradise — Eldorado and Geneva. Both are democracies: in Eldorado everyone is a priest since all they have to do is give thanks, and there are no monks since there is nothing to govern or about which to dispute and intrigue. Since every-

one is of the same opinion — here is the "general will" in
full bloom — people never go to law courts or prisons. But
both men find these comfortable places too uncomfortably
easy, and they leave. Neither Geneva nor Eldorado allows
room for improvement or for real activity. These are places
of rest, even indolence, and sterile life without challenge.
The life there is pleasant, placid, and stagnant rather than
ideal. Where there is nothing even to pray for, there is nothing to work for or live for. As Faust came to know so well,
if, as in Eldorado and Geneva, we have all our human wants
and needs satisfied as they are here, life is at a standstill.
Since there are no real problems, this creates a new problem: boredom. And art and creativity dry up. As Robert
Frost once asked: "How can we in America ever write the
great Russian novel as long as life goes on so unterribly?"
Or, as Sophia Antonovna says to Razumov:

> In life, you see, there is not much choice. You have either
> to rot or to burn. And there is not one of us, painted or
> unpainted, that would not rather burn than rot (250).

The natives of Geneva and Eldorado seem like card-
board cutouts rather than the real, breathing people etched
with acid realism like Voltaire's Cacambo or Conrad's Tekla, who will drudge their lives away extending relief and
compassion to others.

It is somehow poignantly satisfying at the end of each
novel when Candide and his friends retire from all their
searchings to the ordinary round of labors on their little
farm of cultivating their garden, and the broken Razumov
and sacrificial Tekla return to the interior of Russia to a
little wooden house where she tends him unweariedly (379).
This is the realism, the accommodation — and sometimes
the wisdom — that is the end of all philosophy. And the
reader, in each case, gradually learns to make acceptance
of limitations a matter of earned experience rather than

learned dogmas and finely-spun philosophies. As Flaubert wrote to Louise Colet:

> "Thus the end of *Candide* is for me patent proof of a genius of the first water. The claws of the lion are marked on that quiet conclusion, as stupid as life itself." [19]

Perhaps it was actually that sort of thing that Conrad was trying to say some years after the novel's composition when he wrote in the conclusion to the "Author's Note":

> The oppressors and the oppressed are all Russians together; and the world is brought once more face to face with the truth of the saying that the tiger cannot change his stripes nor the leopard his spots.

For, as that passage reads on its own, such a moral-pointing message of social quietism and cosmic fatalism is surely unnecessary to anyone who has read the book itself, which defies cliché-ridden encapsulations to tell a deeply affecting story that with unforgettable acuity poses anew to every reader one of life's larger questions. That is the eternal enigma of how, despite the most committed efforts we can make to live lives of order and purpose, our human condition can be so ruinously vulnerable to vagarious irrational forces that a thinking reed can indeed be broken and a valuable human life become utterly lost.

NOTES

[1] *LG*, p. 235.

[2] *LG*, p. 233.

[3] TS, N20.11-21.2. For the full quote from the typescript, see the essay by David Leon Higdon in this volume.

[4] George L. Kline, "Russian Philosophy," in *The Encyclopedia of Philosophy*, ed. Paul Edwards (New York: Macmillan & The Free Press, 1967), VII:261.

[5] Quoted in George Woodcock and Ivan Avakumovic, *The Anarchist Prince: Peter Kropotkin* (New York: Schocken Books, 1971), p. 347.

[6] Kline, VII, 258. See also James H. Billington, *The Icon and the Axe: An Interpretive History of Russian Culture* (New York: Vintage Books, 1970), p. 310.

[7] *Pensé* 347. See also Hay, p. 292 and David Leon Higdon, "Pascal's *Pensé* 347 in *Under Western Eyes*," *Conradiana*, 5:2 (1973), 81-83.

[8] Billington, p. 310; Kline, VII, 258.

[9] Kline, VII, 258.

[10] Richard H. Popkin, "Skepticism," in *The Encyclopedia of Philosophy*, ed. Paul Edwards (New York: Macmillan & The Free Press, 1967), VII:449.

[11] Popkin, VII:454.

[12] Popkin, VII:453.

[13] Popkin, VII:454.

[14] Billington, p. 325.

[15] Kline, p. 259; Billington, pp. 173, 223, 230.

[16] "Introduction" to Denis Diderot, *Rameau's Nephew* (New York: Penguin, 1966), p. 27.

[17] "Conrad and Rousseau: Concepts of Man and Society," in *Joseph Conrad: A Commemoration*, ed. Norman Sherry (London: Macmillan Press Ltd., 1976), p. 83.

[18] *Lettres françaises*, ed. G. Jean-Aubry (Paris: Gallimard, 1930), p. 144.

[19] Flaubert to Louise Colet, April 24, 1852; quoted in Voltaire, *Candide*, ed. Robert M. Adams (New York: Norton, 1966), p. 189.

"Is he then living actually in Russia" I cried. "All that risk for a peasant girl! Don't you think it's extremely wrong of him to expose his precious person"

Sophia Antonovna preserved a mysterious silence for a while, then ~~before she finally~~ made a statement:

"He just simply adores her!

"Does he? Well. I hope then he won't ~~hesitate~~ to beat him". ~~badly~~

Sophia Antonovna wished me good bye pretending not to have heard a word of my impious hope. But in the very doorway she turned round and declared in a ~~firm new~~ voice:

Peter Ivanovitch is an inspired man".

End. 25 Jan 1910 J.C.